"Through this bo[...] you. He'll show y[...] own strength but by allowing Jesus to lead you, guide you, and protect you. Reading this book and putting these principles into practice will be a real blessing for you."

Tony Dungy, Super Bowl–winning player and coach, from the foreword

"I've had the honor of knowing Vernon for years, and I've witnessed firsthand the strength, resilience, and unwavering faith that have guided him through some of life's hardest moments. What I find most powerful about this book is how Vernon doesn't just share his story; he shows us how courage can help us conquer our own fears in a world filled with uncertainty. I wholeheartedly recommend this book. It's a lifeline for those seeking courage, healing, and the strength to live beyond fear."

Travis Greene, Grammy Award–winning artist; pastor, Forward City Church; author, *Are You Praying for the Wrong Thing?*

"There is no doubt that fear is inevitable. And that feeling is present in everything we do, every environment we are in, and every decision we make. Vernon helps us realize this is all normal. His book does a beautiful job teaching, guiding, and providing clarity on how to maneuver through the range of emotions that fear provokes. His transparency in his own growth as a leader and husband beautifully translates to how he wants us to choose joy over fear and how bravery is something that we all are able to choose. Using the kingdom and faith as the foundation of how we live beyond fear makes this book easy to comprehend, digest, and practice in our own lives. This book is a game changer for any person grappling with life's curveballs and offers solutions to help us live more fulfilling, joyful lives."

Jay Ell Alexander, owner and CEO, The Vaughn Strategy and Black Girls RUN!

"Vernon is the real deal—his life and leadership reflect the very principles he shares in *Life Beyond Fear*. This book isn't just inspirational; it's deeply practical. If you've ever felt stuck or held back by fear, Vernon's words will equip you to take bold steps of faith. I'm grateful for his friendship and even more grateful that the world gets to experience his wisdom through this book!"

Justin Elam, director, Irresistible Church Network

"I count it an honor to have walked through moments of fear in my life with my brother Vernon Gordon by my side. This book is not only timely but a gem that helps us learn to dance with our fear and celebrate its song as a barometer for growth and advancement in life's journey. As that journey continues, it's now a privilege to be able to walk with Vernon's words."

Joshua Boone, Tony, Grammy, and NAACP Image Award–nominated actor/singer

"*Life Beyond Fear* is more than a book; it's a testimony of God's faithfulness in the face of life's hardest battles. Vernon shares his journey with raw honesty, from surviving cancer and enduring surgeries to navigating deep disappointments. Through it all, he found unshakable courage in God's Word, and now he's inviting you to do the same. If fear has ever held you back, this book will remind you that you're never alone and that a life of bold faith and kingdom courage is waiting for you."

Dr. Jackie Greene, founder, Permission World International Women's Group; pastor, Forward City Church; author, *Permission to Live Free*

LIFE BEYOND FEAR

LIFE BEYOND FEAR

Unlocking Kingdom Courage
in a Worry-Filled World

VERNON GORDON

a division of Baker Publishing Group
Grand Rapids, Michigan

© 2025 by Vernon Lee Gordon III

Published by Revell
a division of Baker Publishing Group
Grand Rapids, Michigan
RevellBooks.com

Printed in the United States of America

All rights reserved. No part of this publication may be reproduced, stored in a retrieval system, or transmitted in any form or by any means—for example, electronic, photocopy, recording—without the prior written permission of the publisher. The only exception is brief quotations in printed reviews.

Library of Congress Cataloging-in-Publication Data
Names: Gordon, Vernon, 1988– author
Title: Life beyond fear : unlocking kingdom courage in a worry-filled world / Vernon Gordon.
Description: Grand Rapids, Michigan : Revell, a division of Baker Publishing Group, [2025] | Includes bibliographical references.
Identifiers: LCCN 2025002594 | ISBN 9780800747213 paperback | ISBN 9780800747442 casebound | ISBN 9781493451432 ebook
Subjects: LCSH: Fear—Religious aspects—Christianity | Courage—Religious aspects—Christianity | Peace of mind—Religious aspects—Christianity
Classification: LCC BV4908.5 .G659 2025
LC record available at https://lccn.loc.gov/2025002594

Unless otherwise indicated, Scripture quotations are from the Holy Bible, New International Version®, NIV®. Copyright © 1973, 1978, 1984, 2011 by Biblica, Inc.® Used by permission of Zondervan. All rights reserved worldwide. www.zondervan.com. The "NIV" and "New International Version" are trademarks registered in the United States Patent and Trademark Office by Biblica, Inc.®

Scripture quotations labeled AMP are from the Amplified Bible. Copyright © 2015 by The Lockman Foundation. Used by permission. www.lockman.org

Scripture quotations labeled CEV are from the Contemporary English Version. Copyright © 1991, 1992, 1995 by American Bible Society. Used by permission.

Scripture quotations labeled ESV are from The Holy Bible, English Standard Version® (ESV®). Copyright © 2001 by Crossway, a publishing ministry of Good News Publishers. Used by permission. All rights reserved. ESV Text Edition: 2016

Scripture quotations labeled MSG are from *The Message*. Copyright © 1993, 2002, 2018 by Eugene H. Peterson. Used by permission of NavPress. All rights reserved. Represented by Tyndale House Publishers.

Scripture quotations labeled NKJV are from the New King James Version®. Copyright © 1982 by Thomas Nelson. Used by permission. All rights reserved.

Scripture quotations labeled NLT are from the *Holy Bible*, New Living Translation. Copyright © 1996, 2004, 2015 by Tyndale House Foundation. Used by permission of Tyndale House Publishers, Carol Stream, Illinois 60188. All rights reserved.

Cover design by Derek Thornton, Notch Design

The author is represented by the literary agent Don Gates of The Gates Group.

Baker Publishing Group publications use paper produced from sustainable forestry practices and postconsumer waste whenever possible.

25 26 27 28 29 30 31   7 6 5 4 3 2 1

To my whole world,
Ashley, Madison, and Jackson.
May you know that my greatest joy
is serving you,
here, now, and forever.

Contents

Foreword by Tony Dungy   11

Introduction   15

PART 1 Facing Fear

1. The Bigger They Are, the Quieter They Fall   23
2. The Faces of Fear   40
3. The Breakup   58
4. Fear Is Not Hard to Find   73

PART 2 Becoming Brave

5. Winning the War Against Worry   89
6. What You See Is What You Get   105
7. Somewhere Over the Rainbow   118
8. Power to the People   133

Contents

PART 3 The Great Unknown

   9. No Guts, No Glory   151
10. Higher Ground   163
11. Inside Out   175
12. Don't Quit   187

    Acknowledgments   199
    Notes   201

Foreword

Fear is a normal human emotion. We all have it. Fear shows up in all shapes and sizes. It affects all of us regardless of our ethnicity, gender, or socioeconomic class. Every one of us will come across something that we fear. It may be a fear of heights, a fear of flying, or even something as simple as a fear of speaking in public. It's quite normal to have a fear of death, which is inevitable for all of us. So, the real question is, If we're all going to encounter fears, how do we handle them?

For thirty-one years, I was a player and coach in the National Football League. Sports, particularly football, teach you to overcome fears. In competition you run into situations that could overwhelm you. *Am I going to be good enough to make the team? If I do make the team, how will I play against others who might be bigger and stronger than me? If we get to a really big game with high stakes, how will I perform?* Playing and coaching helped me learn how to handle some of those fears but not all of them.

When our fourth child, Jordan, was born, we learned he had a very rare genetic disease. The doctors told us the condition was so devastating it was doubtful he would live past three or four years of age. This was unknown territory for my wife Lauren and me. That diagnosis immediately shot fear into us. How would we handle it?

The reality is that fear is something you probably will not be able to totally avoid. However, fear is something you can learn to overcome. I have found that the best way to take on fear is with the help and power of Jesus Christ. Jesus came to give us the gift of eternal life by dying on the cross for our sins, but he also came to give us freedom from fear and worry. In John 6, when his disciples were caught in a terrible storm on the Sea of Galilee, Jesus walked out to them and said, "Don't be afraid. I am here!" (v. 20 NLT). Those are great words to remember in any situation.

In *Life Beyond Fear*, you'll find encouragement to face your fears. Vernon Gordon has firsthand experience with this because he has overcome so many fears in his own life. I met Vernon in an airport when I was taking Jordan to the hospital for a surgical procedure. He noticed this young boy with one leg shorter than the other sitting in a wheelchair. He came over to talk to us, and we found that he had gone through many of the same problems and heartaches that Jordan had gone through. Vernon not only encouraged us in the airport, but he came to visit Jordan in the hospital. His counsel and advice to just trust the Lord for Jordan's care were huge for us. And the fact that we could see how Jesus had gotten him through some of the same types of surgeries helped calm our fears. We have remained friends over the years, and Vernon still checks in on Jordan, who is now twenty-four years old and doing great.

Through this book, Vernon will be a counselor and a coach for you. He'll show you how to overcome fear, not by relying on your own strength but by allowing Jesus to lead you, guide you, and protect you. Reading this book and putting these principles into practice will be a real blessing for you. I know it will help you in the areas of your life where you may have worry or fear. Take heart because Jesus has overcome the world!

Tony Dungy, Super Bowl–winning player and coach

Introduction

Fearless!

Sounds admirable, doesn't it?

This one word, when ascribed to someone's character, is not only honoring, it's downright impressive. Fearless people inspire us, mobilize us, challenge us, and model for us a way of living that feels free. The fearless shape culture, language, art, music, sports, business, and politics. The fearless chart new courses by leaving footprints in the sand on a road less traveled so that others may follow their way.

Oh, what it must be like to be fearless.

When we hear *fearless*, we may have a default avatar that comes to mind. Maybe it's the running back who every Sunday runs into three-hundred-pound bodies and seems to love the full-speed clash of flesh and ground. Perhaps it's the artist who stands in front of thousands and hits high notes coupled with dance moves and never misses a beat. Possibly it's the activist, politician, or community leader whose words have shifted a room, a sanctuary, or an entire city. Maybe it's the fighter who got knocked down, took a moment to gather themselves, and decided to keep moving toward their opponent, refusing the white flag, and willing their way to victory. Perhaps it's the surgeon who exercises their precision and poise under extreme pressure to ensure that a life continues to thrive.

If many of us are honest, the examples above are not the only examples of fearlessness we are privileged to witness. Fearlessness reveals itself not only on the largest of stages but also in the smallest situations of our everyday life. The single mom who works multiple jobs to create an environment of love and opportunity for her children. The entrepreneur who has seen failure and still decides to try again. The childhood cancer patient who knows every day requires a recommitment to fight for a future.

Here's the thing about being fearless: The evidence for it is not always the same, and it's not always easily defined, but when you see it, you know it.

Our normal definition of *fearless* is being without fear or free from fear. Sounds simple enough and to the point. But there is only one problem. I have interviewed hundreds of fearless people—athletes, artists, entrepreneurs, pastors, survivors, and activists—and here's what they all had in common: fear. Each one of them seems to be fearless. And yet, when asked how they do it, they all highlight fear as a part of their journey. They wrote the song scared, couldn't sleep before the speech, or threw up prior to the big game.

It is from this realization that I began to rethink my idea of fearlessness. Maybe, just maybe, fearlessness is not about erasing fears but facing them. Perhaps it's about finding the language, strategies, and solutions to live a life beyond fear—and finding the courage we need to live within our worry-filled world.

As I wrestled with these thoughts, I turned my attention to Scripture to see how the fearless show up. You've probably heard some of these stories, and if you are a Christian, maybe

Introduction

you grew up reading about these men in Sunday school like I did.

Gideon was fearless—if you only read the part of his story when he wins the battle over their enemies. But before that, he's full of fear and self-doubt.

David was fearless—if you only look at him throwing a stone at Goliath. But what about when Saul is chasing him and he finds himself in a cave writing songs of fear and lament?

Joshua was fearless—if you're only considering the Battle of Jericho. But then why does God have to repeatedly tell him to be strong and courageous prior to the start of his leadership journey?

Time and time again, we see the fearless facing fear. What does this mean for our lives in the present? If you ask me, it's simple. We need a response to fear that fosters a future of forward progress. Fear is not our biggest problem; how to face it is.

Did you know that the most repeated command by God in Scripture is "Fear not"? Over and over again, God whispers, speaks, and even shouts to people, "Do not be afraid!" This is sobering. The only reasonable question to ask is: Why does he have to keep repeating himself?

There are over five hundred references in the Bible to fear being the cause of delayed purpose and obedience. From the front cover to the back, you bump into communities that are trying to determine how to leave a legacy. Individuals who are trying to overcome past trauma to find future favor. And even heroes and cowards, who either embraced bravery or fostered fear.

Fear got in the way a lot back then, just as it does now. And I wonder if God might be repeating the same thing from generation to generation: "Fear not! Do not be afraid! Go for it! Take the leap! Make a move! Take the hill! Reach up and grab it! Jump!" Say it however you want, the charge remains the same: Stop standing still and face your fears.

What if the only thing standing in between the life you desire and the life you've been designed for is your bravery?

■ ■ ■

Perhaps you are wondering why I would write this book. I mean, there are plenty of books on fear, faith, and worry. Well, the answer is simple: It's the story I've lived. My story of facing fear began at ten years old.

As a youngster, I was diagnosed with osteogenic sarcoma, an aggressive form of bone cancer that has been known to take the lives of many who have faced it. This discovery revealed two tumors and initiated a journey that involved three years of chemotherapy, the removal of the bones in my right leg from my knee to thigh, and the prognosis of death at least three times. It also required surgery almost every year until I was twenty-two years old.

At the time of this writing, I just had my fourteenth surgery. The fourteenth one, unlike the others, took me by surprise, causing an entirely new set of fears, frustrations, and emotions. I know firsthand what it feels like to worry my way out of difficult work and to wander my way into the wilderness. I know firsthand what it's like to ask big questions and have to make do with small answers. I know firsthand what it's like to be fighting for your present and feel like there's no time for thinking of the future. I know what it's like to feel fear in your heart and have to put a smile on your face because people depend on you. What it's like to choose silence in a storm because you know that if you speak, every word will plant seeds of worry.

Living a worry-filled life robs us of all the great gifts that exist around us—love, joy, kindness, family, generosity, and more. What worry does is blindfold us to the beauty around us. We can feel the anxiety of not knowing what's next, but we can also see the reality of what is in the present.

Within this book, we will explore the data surrounding worry in our culture and look at how this single state can overtake our lives and fuel our fear unless we are intentional about becoming brave. To make it plain, the choice to be brave only exists because fear exists. And fear only grows when it's watered with worry. We can't address worry if we don't address what our worry feeds. Likewise, we can't cultivate bravery without the fight against fear.

Together, we will take a serious look at the challenges and opportunities that show up in our lives in order to build from a brave place. We will consider research and present trends that are relevant to our coming journeys. Additionally, we will explore a broad scope of interdisciplinary contributions, both from modern culture as well as from the timeless truths of Scripture. Finally, we will read a myriad of personal stories that will aid in the discovery of a brave new world for us and those we love.

Throughout my life, I've become all too acquainted with fear. But that's not where my story ends. And it doesn't have to be your storyline either. Here's the hard truth: Fear is inevitable, but bravery is a choice. A choice that can revolutionize your life.

My invitation to you is simple: Choose courage—because your life, your heart, and your future depend on it. Let's take this journey together to the other side of our fears and become brave in a worry-filled world.

PART 1
FACING FEAR

ONE

The Bigger They Are, the Quieter They Fall

"Daddy, I'm writing a book." These were the words of my then-seven-year-old son.

My wife and I had just returned from a vacation in Mexico. We were exhausted from a day of travel. I initially responded with an affirming grunt to let him know: *Daddy hears you—* but I wasn't listening. He repositioned himself in my line of sight. I couldn't help but notice the stack of papers in his hands. I could now see that he didn't want my general affirmation but my undivided attention.

Convicted, I obliged and asked, "What's the name of your book, Jackson?" He responded, "*The Heroics*." I could tell he was eager to share more because he rocks side to side when he's really excited.

Jackson doesn't get excited about much, so I leaned in and said, "Tell me about it."

Jackson began by telling me of his main characters, the Heroics: three superheroes who possess, you guessed it, superpowers. Par for the course, except for the fact that one of them was a YouTuber—that was his superpower. The others were pretty standard hero material, with superstrength or superintelligence. They would eventually be joined by a hero with superspeed, and the four of them would be pitted against a villain—because heroes are made by villains.

As a dad, I was impressed by the characters and plotline alone, but Jackson took things a step further. He outlined it all into a chapter book—beginning with "The Origin" and ending with "The Epilogue." "The Epilogue," really? He's seven. If that wasn't enough, he had also started illustrating the book, section by section, providing supporting imagery to accessorize the storyline of *The Heroics*. (Okay, at this point I was all in.) I was a cross between a proud dad and an ambitious coach, ready to celebrate him no matter what but also ready to lead him to the release of this idea in his heart.

As I looked through the illustrations, one thing struck me. It was obvious that in every picture, the villain was huge. The villain towered over the heroes, and the only path to victory was through this massive opponent.

When I asked Jackson why the villain was so big, he didn't have a response. It was almost as if he assumed that's just the way it always is. It dawned on me: The enemy has to be *big* because that's what makes the story. To overcome, to be victorious, to beat all the odds, there has to be a contrast between the size of your story and your struggle.

The Avengers need Thanos.

Simba needs Scar.

Mario needs Bowser.

Harry Potter needs Lord Voldemort.
Luke Skywalker needs Darth Vader.
Michael Jordan needs the "Bad Boy" Pistons.
Ethan Hunt needs the impossible.

Legends are born because giants, or giant circumstances, exist. Because giants create the scenes in which our superpowers can emerge.

Fear manifests itself as the giant appearing in our lives. But fear is a form of both opposition and opportunity. It is both a wall and a bridge. A problem and a promotion. Where we find fear, we often find a foretaste of our future.

When we learn to see fear as an alert, it allows for a new attitude and an alternate approach on how to face the giants of life. We can't get the strategy right if we're seeing the struggle wrong. Yes, facing fear requires a strategy. We shouldn't haphazardly jump into a fight without knowing a way to win. Fear can be conquered, silenced, and forced into submission if we have the right strategy.

I couldn't shake the size of the giant in my son's illustrations. It was telling me how we view life's biggest obstacles. Not only did it suggest how we see what we face, it revealed how we see ourselves when facing it. The Heroics were superstrong, superfast, and superintelligent. If we are not careful, we might simply think the solution to big problems is more strength, faster decisions, and wiser actions. But this is not the way.

In all fairness, movies, social media, and folktales have offered us a singular picture of what bravery looks like, sounds like, and wins like when facing life's biggest fears. If we were building the avatar, it would be someone who is physically strong and tall, outspoken and well-spoken, kind and just, wise and resourceful. We're talking MacGyver, Tony Stark, Rocky Balboa stuff. Or in real life, The Rock, Michael B.

Jordan, LeBron James, Tom Brady, Barack Obama stuff. Now, if I could only grow six inches, work out three times a day, become handy, add a few *M*'s to my bank account, and achieve a mass following, I'll be ready to step into the brave season of my life.

Of course, I highlight these adjectives and public figures lightheartedly. If you want to build huge biceps and practice front rolls on the living room carpet for the event of a fight against ninjas breaking out at your local coffee shop, I'm all for it. But the reality remains that bravery and heroism in American culture are typecast. The consequence? We neglect becoming the hero of our own story, let alone someone else's, because we don't feel that we fit the part.

The truth is we platform a version of victory and bravery that is often inconsistent with both faith and fulfillment. There is a common cultural colloquialism that reinforces this incomplete narrative of self-pursuit and false empowerment: The bigger they are, the harder they fall.

While widely used now, many credit British boxer Robert Fitzsimmons with its origin prior to a fight in the early 1900s. Fitzsimmons was an accomplished fighter, becoming a champion in three different divisions. But what makes his story interesting is that he holds a Guinness world record as the lightest heavyweight champion ever, weighing in at just 165 pounds when he won the title. It was his size and weight, his unsuspecting frame, that caused many to doubt both his abilities and his odds at victory. And yet, when asked about how he'd face the giants of his day in combat, he ushered these words into existence: "The bigger they are, the harder they fall."

There's just one problem. There's no ring for fighting fear. No pay-per-view event. No roaring audience encouraging us to pick our confidence up off the mat. No corner man to patch us up in between one hard meeting and the next. No, the fight against fear often occurs in the quiet car rides from one destination to another. It's fought in tabs and folders that contain drafts of world-shifting ideas and proposals that never get sent. It's fought in the private conversations of self-doubt and pessimism that prevent us from stepping out into the possibilities of our future. It's fought on the pages of social media that cause us to think less of our purpose because of comparisons to someone else's platform.

This all adds up to a sobering reality about fighting fear: The bigger they are, the quieter they fall. People rarely see or hear the fall of fear—they just experience the benefits of it. People will experience the gift, but they don't see the grit that person needed to gain an inch in their purpose. They will celebrate the launch of the initiative but aren't privy to the monthslong battle won against personal insecurity. People will experience the business or nonprofit but they didn't see the war won against worry. People will experience the impact of the speech but weren't there when the speaker overcame the dialogue with doubt. Fears fall quietly, but the fruit is seen publicly.

Considering this reality, maybe the healthiest and most sustainable way to build bravery into our life is not by projecting strength, speed, or smarts. I'm most certainly not suggesting that those traits aren't also valuable assets to the journey of life. But what if there was one habit you could implement in your daily rhythms that could help you live a life beyond fear in a worry-filled world? One habit that would fuel your faith in facing fears time and time again?

What's that one habit, you ask? I'll tell you in just a second. But first, let's talk about why we should focus on our habits.

Hear me loud and clear: Hope is not enough. Those were the words, give or take a few, that I heard when entering physical therapy for what felt like the hundredth time as a young cancer patient. Surgery was an almost-every-other-year family activity at this point. And physical therapists have come to be my favorite physicians. This particular day, an inquiry was made as to whether I'd been doing my exercises at home. And while I certainly had every intention of using the gift of gab to fabricate the degree of my faithfulness toward the process, the numbers didn't lie. It was evident that I was hopeful for a full recovery but had failed to apply any healthy habits to make that hope possible. The result? Delayed progress and physical frustration.

The hard truth is that hope is a beautiful friend but a horrible spouse. Date your hopes, marry your habits. I'm all for hope. As a matter of fact, I've often said my life's purpose is to be a communicator of hope. However, hope is the catalyst for change, but habits are the sustainer of it. High hopes with low habits are an invitation to cycles, not change.

If there's anybody who models bravery beyond their circumstances in the Bible, it's a guy named David. His battle with Goliath has become not only a pillar to the Christian community but a societal symbol of all of the benefits of facing fears. Unfortunately, like with most things in our society, we desire to skip to the good part. However, David's story is not only highlights. Rather, we find a story that starts long before he ever stepped foot on the battleground with Goliath. It would benefit us all to see the full story, so let's go back to the beginning.

We are first introduced to David in 1 Samuel 16. At the time, he's not the central character. The prophet Samuel has been tasked with anointing the next king of Israel and is led to the house of Jesse. Upon learning this, Jesse lines up all his sons with pride. All except David.

> When they arrived, Samuel saw Eliab and thought, "Surely the Lord's anointed stands here before the Lord."
> But the Lord said to Samuel, "Do not consider his appearance or his height, for I have rejected him. The Lord does not look at the things people look at. People look at the outward appearance, but the Lord looks at the heart."
> Then Jesse called Abinadab and had him pass in front of Samuel. But Samuel said, "The Lord has not chosen this one either." Jesse then had Shammah pass by, but Samuel said, "Nor has the Lord chosen this one." Jesse had seven of his sons pass before Samuel, but Samuel said to him, "The Lord has not chosen these." So he asked Jesse, "Are these all the sons you have?"
> "There is still the youngest," Jesse answered. "He is tending the sheep."
> Samuel said, "Send for him; we will not sit down until he arrives."
> So he sent for him and had him brought in. He was glowing with health and had a fine appearance and handsome features.
> Then the Lord said, "Rise and anoint him; this is the one." (vv. 6–12)

Can you imagine the shock? Jesse is convinced that it could not possibly be his youngest son, so much so that he hasn't even invited him to the ceremony. This marks the first fight David encounters—not with people but with confidence. There's a certain insecurity that can live in us when we know we weren't considered or were passed over for an opportunity, and by family, no less. And yet the story continues.

Sometime later, the people of Israel would get in a battle against the Philistines, who were, by many standards, a far superior army. Jesse, still without regard for David's true potential, sends him to the battlefield to take lunch to his brothers, where David finds a standoff between the two armies. It was the custom of the time that two armies could each send out a representative for one conclusive duel to decide the fates of two entire nations.

Goliath was the champion of the Philistines. I imagine him looking like André the Giant, Shaquille O'Neal, or Mr. T. For clarity, that's not biblically verified but the product of my theological imagination. Nonetheless, the Bible goes to great lengths to highlight Goliath's size, strength, and extensive war experience, implying he's highly favored to win. Consequently, nobody is volunteering for this fight.

In steps David, and as he overhears this exchange, he volunteers to represent his entire nation in a fight to the death. It is at this point that he's brought to Saul, the current king:

> David said to Saul, "Let no one lose heart on account of this Philistine; your servant will go and fight him."
>
> Saul replied, "You are not able to go out against this Philistine and fight him; you are only a young man, and he has been a warrior from his youth."
>
> But David said to Saul, "Your servant has been keeping his father's sheep. When a lion or a bear came and carried off a sheep from the flock, I went after it, struck it and rescued the sheep from its mouth. When it turned on me, I seized it by its hair, struck it and killed it. Your servant has killed both the lion and the bear; this uncircumcised Philistine will be like one of them, because he has defied the armies of the living God. The Lord who rescued me from the paw of the lion and the paw of the bear will rescue me from the hand of this Philistine."
>
> Saul said to David, "Go, and the Lord be with you."
>
> Then Saul dressed David in his own tunic. He put a coat of armor on him and a bronze helmet on his head. David

fastened on his sword over the tunic and tried walking around, because he was not used to them.

"I cannot go in these," he said to Saul, "because I am not used to them." So he took them off. Then he took his staff in his hand, chose five smooth stones from the stream, put them in the pouch of his shepherd's bag and, with his sling in his hand, approached the Philistine. (1 Sam. 17:31–40)

Yet again we see the fight before the fight. David is told by his leader: There's no way you can do this. It's seen as not only unwise but seemingly impossible. Consequently, he finds himself dressed in the king's armor—an attempt to look the part or present as one who can handle the moment. This is often what happens when fear shows up in our journey. We first think about how courage looks before we properly assess how courage lives. But most greatness is about not what was copied but rather what was created.

Interestingly enough, David's response to Saul is the confirmation of this chapter's key principle. Hope is one thing; habits are another. He's saying to Saul, "I've fought lions and I've fought bears, and this giant is just like one of them." In other words, "I've made a life of practicing this skill in the dark, so this moment is nothing more than the same skill coming to the light."

David's fear fell when no one was watching. There was no one there when he faced fear and rescued his first sheep. There was no one there when he faced fear with the lion or the bear. There was no one there when he faced his family who didn't believe in him. His fears fell where no one could see. What seemed like a fearless boy going into battle was really the by-product of big fears falling in quiet places. Because the bigger they are, the quieter they fall.

So, if there is only one habit you could implement in your weekly rhythms to stay brave, here it is: failure. You read that right! I'm telling you that you should try something you could fail at every week. The practice of institutionalizing failure into your human experience will enable your mindset and emotions to better handle fear's lies and limits. It is the practice of looking for failure instead of always waiting for it to find you.

Now, I know what you're thinking. *Vernon, everything about that sounds wrong. I'm not reading a book about facing fear to find failure. I bought this book to find freedom, faith, fruit, and to feel better. But the last thing I expected was to find failure.* But what if the failure you've been avoiding is actually designed to give you access to the other side? What if failure could be your friend?

When I was a teenager, I recall someone gifting me a poster that spoke to this truth. Maybe you've seen it before. It presents the faces of six world-changing leaders. Next to each of their faces is a paragraph not about their successes but about, you guessed it, their failures. Michael Jordan had this to say on that poster: "I've missed more than 9,000 shots in my career. I've lost almost 300 games. 26 times, I've been trusted to take the game winning shot and missed. I've failed over and over and over again in my life. And that is why I succeed."

This prompted me to begin studying not only the success of great leaders but what preceded it. And I found that Jordan wasn't alone. The Wright brothers had multiple plane crashes. Steven Spielberg was rejected from film school three times. Henry Ford's first two car companies failed. Sir James Dyson suffered through 5,126 failed prototypes before he landed on the first working Dyson vacuum. Colonel Harland Sanders of KFC was rejected over one thousand times before finding a franchise partner.

Nobody thinks of that when we're eating great chicken. Nobody thinks of the companies that failed when we hear a commercial say, "Built Ford Tough." We eat the chicken, use the vacuum, get on the plane, watch the groundbreaking movies, and call Jordan the greatest basketball player of all time—because their failures come second to their successes.

Why does this matter? Research has proven that the fear of failure is one of the strongest influences on the human experience. We'll talk more about this research in coming chapters, but for many, we don't fear the fear itself as much as we fear the loss of image, influence, or opportunity that may happen if the fear proves to be true. Let me say it another way. The question is: If there was nothing to lose, what would you do? But that's not the reality, and we all know it. There is something to lose. However, as we just saw, there's also something to gain when we can leverage failure as a tool and not a trial.

In weightlifting, there's this principle called lifting until failure. In this process, you don't set a limit when you start. Rather, you continue to press the weight, repetition after repetition, until you exhaust the muscle group you're working on beyond your perceived limits. Anatomically, when we lift weights, we intentionally break down our muscle fibers, creating microscopic tears. Consequently, our body not only repairs the damage done but begins growing new muscle tissue as a reaction. Failure is a positive part of your future, if you know how to use it.

And all this is happening beneath the surface, in the corner of the early morning gym, in the basement, where the dropping of each weight reverberates off the concrete walls. And the strongest, biggest, and most impressive summer bodies are this chapter's truth in motion: The bigger they are, the quieter they fall.

Here are three practical ways to incorporate healthy failure into your weekly rhythm. This is not an exhaustive list, and I encourage you to seek other ways to practice the gift of life beyond fear. However, I hope that you'll begin to see these as starting points to creating a healthy habit.

Set Stretch Goals

Often in leadership circles, I've encountered a simple yet challenging question. I've even heard it lace the words of artists and poets alike. And every time I hear it, I'm drawn to reconsider my ways and my work. What's the question? "When was the last time you did something for the first time?"

When was the last time you had a goal, dream, or aspiration that would require you to be a stronger version of yourself? When was the last time you set out to accomplish something uncomfortable? When was the last time something moved you beyond your current capabilities, and the only way forward was to stretch? When we set goals and never readjust them or revisit them, we actually risk losing strength. We must reframe the purpose of goal-setting. Goals are most commonly known for what they call us to reach, which I agree is necessary. But they also can provide a healthy push against the mundanity of life. If you have big enough goals, they will require failures.

Suppose that every goal you set, you immediately accomplished. In that case, it may suggest that not only was the goal not challenging enough but you possibly missed the opportunity to grow stronger in the process. Seeking and setting goals that intentionally have both a standard level and a stretch level of achievement ensures we are always pushing beyond the familiar.

In my life, I usually divide goals into four categories: personal, professional, spiritual, and familial. This ensures that each goal stretches me to my highest possible potential. And every year, there are some that I don't reach. The disappointments, the failures, and the falls I experience in each of these categories build my capacity for and comfort with the aforementioned adjectives. While they aren't emotionally catastrophic losses, they are revealing losses that serve to familiarize my heart with the ever-existing tension between falling short and pursuing my personal best. Here are a few of my goals that are currently stretching me:

- Golfing: Trying to break 90. This game is challenging, and it keeps me humble.
- Cooking: I try a new recipe once a month that doesn't always turn out the way I expected.
- Riding a bike: With my history of surgeries, I have not been able to ride a bike since childhood. It's my goal to accomplish this by the end of this year.
- Family time: Be at the dinner table three nights a week without my phone.

Maybe these don't seem like much to you, or perhaps they even seem insignificant, but each of them is hard for me. And by working the muscle of disappointment, failure, and resistance in my life, it keeps me hungry to build the power to overcome them.

Practice Contentment

In 2016, our church took its first corporate mission trip. If you've ever known someone who's done international missions, the statements I am about to make won't be foreign. You arrive with thoughts of helping, serving, and providing needed aid to less fortunate communities. But it never fails: Those who went to serve are moved to not only compassion but reflection and introspection. You leave saying they helped you more than you helped them. You still see poverty, pain, and the struggle of a world beyond your belief. But you also see pride, perseverance, and people's ability to still have joy in spite of unbelievable circumstances.

Those who have traveled to places where they've been in proximity to pain find it easier to process loss and inconvenience in their own life. But the truth is that you don't have to travel internationally to feel this: There are stories, experiences, and communities all around us that provide this type of perspective.

Engaging in these environments is vital to a pure heart. They allow us not only to serve but to learn and see resilience in daily living. Ultimately, this positions us to cultivate these skills in our own lives. Often, we find that the practices and compromises we must make to fully engage in these moments reshape our own perceived priorities and preferences. This goes against our comforts and produces a daily resilience that becomes a reference point when we must endure our own seasons of difficulty.

This type of failure chisels away at one of our culture's greatest personal prisons: public image. The idea that we can project ourselves as being without failure, without fear, or without frailty is an illusion. And yet, it plays out day after day on social media timelines fueled by filters and not by truth. One way we fight this falsehood in our lives is by allowing ourselves to be seen not for all we have but for what we don't. Practicing limitations and embracing the act of being satisfied with less are righteous rebellions in and of themselves.

This practice also has the potential to unleash new measures of productivity and perspective in our life. Throughout history, we've seen limited resources spark creativity and ingenuity. It's like the old proverb says: "Necessity is the mother of innovation." The key to unlocking our future could be found outside of the comforts we refuse to release. See what the practice of minimalism can produce in your life.

Pursue Diversity of Thought

Diversity is a term used for many purposes, most of which I believe to be pure and purposeful. Whenever we think about diversity, we tend to think of a specific type of person or set of individuals, and rightfully so, as that's a general application. Diversity shows up in many categories, such as ethnicity, economic status, and gender. But there are certainly other forms of diversity worth consideration, such as physical ability and disability, religion, and age. The point is this: There are a lot of different people with different windows into our world. Our ability to converse with those who don't simply provide confirmation bias but instead offer unique and broadening perspectives to our purview is vital to our ability to face our fears.

So why don't we pursue it more? Simple: It's complicated. As much as we proclaim a desire for growth in our society, we like things and people that don't push back on our comforts and adopted commentary. It's just plain ole easier to feed our fears than to fight them. To say what we've always said, see what we've always seen, and believe what we've always believed.

Over the last several years, we've heard many thoughts aimed across airways and dinner tables alike. One response could be to simply retreat to those who think like us and process the world through our personal preferences. Or we could leverage the diversity of thought around us to stretch our perspectives, thus enabling our lives to be a deeper reflection of empathy and advocacy.

But don't be deceived. Diversity of thought around us almost always creates an inner tension that does not quickly dissolve. Whether politically, socially, or personally, we all need those around us who push our thoughts to the limits. The alternative is a lived experience that is driven by our fears and not our future. In a future chapter, we'll talk more about this—in particular, how racism, sexism, and classism are fueled by destructive thought patterns that limit our ability to live whole and free. When it's all said and done, diversity of thought can produce less fear and more faith in the human experience.

Not convinced on the case for failure? I can understand that. But consider one of the most powerful examples of this truth, found in the journey of J. K. Rowling, the author of the famed world of Harry Potter. When she was writing the first book in the series, she was a single mother, unemployed, and considering suicide. She struggled to get *Harry Potter and the Philosopher's Stone* published. It was rejected by almost every major publisher in the United Kingdom, until a small publisher agreed to publish it—reluctantly, might I add.

In 2008, Rowling was the commencement speaker for Harvard's graduation and shared these words:

> So why do I talk about the benefits of failure? Simply because failure meant a stripping away of the inessential. I stopped pretending to myself that I was anything other than what I was, and began to direct all my energy into finishing the only work that mattered to me. Had I really succeeded at anything else, I might never have found the determination to succeed in the one arena I believed I truly belonged. I was set free, because my greatest fear had been realized, and I was still alive. . . . And so rock bottom became the solid foundation on which I rebuilt my life.
>
> You might never fail on the scale I did, but some failure in life is inevitable. It is impossible to live without failing at something, unless you live so cautiously that you might as

well not have lived at all—in which case, you fail by default. Failure gave me an inner security that I had never attained by passing examinations. Failure taught me things about myself that I could have learned no other way.[1]

So you see, stretching our limits, pushing against the pressure of public image, and allowing thought diversity to enter our lives give us the best opportunity to live beyond fear's grasp. Make no mistake about it: Fear grows when we feed it. However, when we face it, piece by piece, moment by moment, we take back our life. But don't be alarmed when victory doesn't seem visible. Because the bigger they are, the quieter they fall.

TWO

The Faces of Fear

Can we all agree that movie sequels are not always for the best?
 Like, we can really ruin some great movie moments by trying to remake the magic. Now, let me tell you why this is a passion point for me. For anyone who knows me, they know that watching movies is my favorite thing to do for rest. Give me a day off or a week off, and you can find me on the couch, wrapped up in a blanket, extra-butter popcorn to my left, a large Coke with ice filled to the brim in the biggest cup in the house to my right. And don't forget the TV turned to volume 80. Now, if my wife is home, this picture may get slightly modified to a big Stanley cup of water and the volume reduced to 30, but we don't have to get into that right now. The point is, movies are my thing.
 Movies help my mind recover, slow my thoughts down, and transport me to a world of fantasy, romance, education,

or espionage that is healthy for my soul. The storylines, plot twists, and character arcs pull me in. I love movies. But if there's one thing I loathe, it's messing up a strong story with a weak sequel. It's hard to keep a story going, particularly a good one. However, every now and then they get it right.

Mission: Impossible is one of my favorite movie franchises of all time. With every release, they seem to add layers to Ethan Hunt and the IMF team that keep me fully engaged. *Mission: Impossible 2* is one of my favorites. In this installment, they establish an unmistakable tension from the very first scene in the movie.

Ethan Hunt and a notable scientist are sitting next to each other on a plane. The scientist is transporting information about a deadly virus that could harm millions of people if released. A conversation ensues, and then in an unexpected turn of events, Ethan assaults the man and takes the briefcase. After a moment of shock for the viewer, it is revealed that Ethan Hunt is not actually Ethan Hunt. It's the primary antagonist wearing a facial mask that allows him to assume Ethan's identity and voice. From this point forward in the film, you see a series of faces worn by multiple characters, and you're never quite sure who is who. What these masks bring to the film is an undeniable curiosity to every moment with an underlying question: "What am I really looking at?"

In many ways, I think that's the question of life as well, especially when it comes to fear and its presence in our life. "What am I really looking at?" Very often we can go through an entire conversation, or even an entire season, never recognizing that we're speaking to fear because the face that it wears masks its true intentions. If we're going to face fear, we must first become more aware of the many faces it assumes.

Your mission, should you choose to accept it, is to discern the faces of fear that may be present in your life and to discover how they may be impacting your day-to-day reality.

Okay, I get it, I get it; the *Mission: Impossible* thing was too much there, but I couldn't resist. Nonetheless, the mission remains the same. We must discover the faces fear wears in our life and how we can develop strategies to avoid fear-based decision-making, which is a dangerous way to live.

This has been the call to and the challenge of all of humanity since the beginning of time. In Genesis, we see the first face of fear appear. Adam and Eve are living in the garden, lacking for nothing. They are fully known to God, each other, and themselves. It's what we all hope for and the ideal God desired since the beginning. Then the serpent appears and begins a conversation, grounded on one simple question.

> Now the serpent was more crafty than any of the wild animals the LORD God had made. He said to the woman, "Did God really say, 'You must not eat from any tree in the garden'?"
>
> The woman said to the serpent, "We may eat fruit from the trees in the garden, but God did say, 'You must not eat fruit from the tree that is in the middle of the garden, and you must not touch it, or you will die.'"
>
> "You will not certainly die," the serpent said to the woman. "For God knows that when you eat from it your eyes will be opened, and you will be like God, knowing good and evil."
>
> When the woman saw that the fruit of the tree was good for food and pleasing to the eye, and also desirable for gaining wisdom, she took some and ate it. She also gave some to her husband, who was with her, and he ate it. Then the eyes of both of them were opened, and they realized they were naked; so they sewed fig leaves together and made coverings for themselves. (Gen. 3:1–7)

There's a lot we need to unpack here. If you would indulge me, let's put a pin there and take the scenic route before returning. I believe that once we get back, we'll have a fresh lens on how to discern what's happening in this text and in many others like it.

As a hospital kid, I learned very early the rhythm and rhetoric of medical professionals. In particular, every visit is rooted in three primary objectives. The first objective is to determine a diagnosis—simply put, what's actually going on here. In my experience, this is the longest and most frustrating part. The best medical professionals are patient, meticulous, and simultaneously sensitive to your urgency to find answers. But it is a balancing act.

Consider that what we share as patients and what's first seen by doctors are merely symptoms. This sets off a battery of questions and tests, as the doctors rely on their experience to quickly identify the root cause of our issue. All of this while managing the tension not to jump to premature diagnoses, which is also dangerous.

We've all probably heard of or maybe experienced firsthand instances when someone was minimized or misdiagnosed, causing more serious issues to emerge. It's for this reason that this first phase is so vital to properly determine what's actually going on instead of simply solving the symptoms, which is particularly easy in today's world of medicine. We can mute the cough and miss the cancer. We can numb the pain and miss the fracture. We can hide the scar and leave the pain. But we don't go to doctors to solve the symptoms; we go so they can find the source.

Following the diagnosis, things move pretty quickly. A treatment plan is established—a series of actions that if followed should result in a specific outcome. Which is the third objective: a prognosis, or predicted outcome based on their understanding of the diagnosis and the treatment prescribed.

Here's what I've come to find: We pursue this type of clarity for our physical health but neglect it in our spiritual health.

We are satisfied with singing, sermons, scrolling social media, and anything else that satisfies our symptoms. But when we take the time and effort to properly identify what's really going on here, it changes our future in ways we can't imagine.

So let's go back to Genesis with this filter in mind. I feel most Christians believe that Eve fell to the deception of the serpent, and I've heard several theories as to why. She wanted to be like God. It was a test of free will because how can you love God if you don't have to choose God? She was enticed by the ability to be a better version of herself. Let me be clear: I think the hermeneutics surrounding those thoughts are sound in some ways, but if you ask me, she was afraid. It's that simple. And the text says, "her husband, who was with her," meaning Adam, so more accurately, *they* were afraid (v. 6).

Eating the fruit is the symptom, but the motivation is simple: *What if I'm missing out?* The fear of missing out is found in Genesis from the beginning. Adam and Eve began to wonder: *What if there's more that I could have? What if there's more that I could do? What if there's more that I could become?* And these thoughts prompt actions that are damaging to their wholeness and health.

If we're honest, that same voice has shown up in many of our lives. For some of us it's still and small, and for others it's loud and obnoxious. Here's the danger: We can label it whatever we want. We may call it a drive, a dream, or the pursuit of wisdom. We can even call it worship. And all these things are certainly essential and to be celebrated when accurately at work. But if we're labeling them wrong and we're enabling our fears to make decisions about our future, we can end up in the same predicament: a fall.

Notice that from the moment fear takes root, Eve sees everything differently. What once prompted a response about what God said now is all about what she sees: "When the woman saw that the fruit of the tree was good for food and pleasing to the eye, and also desirable for gaining wisdom, she took some and ate it" (v. 6).

This is the same tree she said a few verses earlier was off-limits. When we don't properly identify fear, it drives us to decisions that seem simple and harmless but are dangerous and debilitating to our future.

Fear is not after your future; it's after your decisions. Because daily decisions determine future possibilities. If I desire to be debt-free in the future, that means my decisions today about my spending are crucial. If I desire to change my body composition and appearance in the future, then my decisions today about my eating and exercise are crucial. If I desire to raise children who are ready for the world beyond my home in the future, then my decisions today about the lessons I share and exposure I allow are crucial. And the list goes on.

This is the place where fear is most dangerous, primarily because it's most undetected in our daily dialogues, responses, behaviors, interpretations, and decisions. Taking inventory of these small exchanges can reveal fear at work on our heart, relationships, and desired future. Most of our mental pictures about facing fear look like the closing fight scene at the end of an action movie. Consequently, we heard the roar, but we missed the whispers. We saw the giant, but we missed the spy. We felt the storm, but we missed the clouds. In other words, it was always there, working against us, and by the time we noticed it, it was bigger than we had bargained for.

So, how do we notice it? How do we name it? How do we fight it?

■ ■ ■

It had been one of those days full of laughs and spontaneous adventures in Columbia, South Carolina, during one recent summer. This led to an evening with no agenda, just random topics of conversation, good food, and relaxation. We were visiting our friends Travis and Jackie, and Jackie is always asking insightful questions. She's one of those people who seem to care about the layer beneath the surface that we often never unveil to people. Without hesitation, she asked me a question I had never been asked before.

"Vernon, what is life like on the other side of cancer?"

Without hesitation, I was about to offer what I felt was a reasonable and expedient response. One that I thought would sound measured, full of gratitude and grit. And then I paused and began to contemplate for what felt like fifteen minutes, even though it was probably only thirty seconds. And then I said, "It's managing fears and fighting to experience the best of life every day."

If I'm being honest, I was surprised at my own response, as I surely thought the appropriate answer would be much lighter in tone and take. However, that was probably the truest answer I had, and I'll tell you why.

When you enter remission, your paperwork, people—even your social media posts—all point to being done with cancer. It is a moment that says cancer is no longer in you. And that is certainly worthy of celebration. But just because cancer is no longer in you doesn't mean it's no longer affecting you. There are quite often what they call late effects, symptoms that can emerge in multiple areas of your health as a result of chemotherapy, radiation, and other forms of treatment.

To put this in perspective, the paperwork that detailed my late effects was five pages long, front and back. It highlighted the potential for diminished hearing, heart issues, infertility, arthritis, liver issues, and of course the risk of various cancers returning. So when I cough for a week, there's the thought: *Is it lung cancer?* Or when I feel a pain in my leg, I'm left to wonder: *Is this age or is this more?* Those thoughts, those effects, those constant reminders of "what if" are ever-present fears that emerge in my daily life. And for most who've overcome cancer, they will tell you there's a general cloud of fear hanging over every doctor's visit, sickly moment, or late-night thought of *I hope this isn't that.*

One day, I was deliberating with my family about my interest in hiking and how there was some risk involved due to my physical condition. I told them then, and I tell you now, "I'm not going to live like I'm dying." Fear is a constant reality, but it doesn't have to be the star of the show. I choose every day to put it in the background, an extra in the crowd, limiting its influence on my heart, habits, and hopes. But that didn't happen overnight. Through great friendships, talk therapy, and my faith, I found that fear was often hiding in my life with a different face. Learning how to identify it and influence it has made a world of difference.

Growing up in down-home Chesapeake, Virginia, they'd say it's time to "nip this in the bud." But before we step into this shared battle, we need shared language. I've come to find that fear's presence is both diverse and covert, which has prompted me to categorize eight faces of fear. They are various expressions and forms that emerge in my life seasonally and strategically to hinder my hope. Now, before we take a look at the eight faces of fear, it's important to note that while you may readily notice some of the faces, others may be a surprise to you. My encouragement is not to be too quick to dismiss any of them. After careful consideration, you may find one that shows up more than you think.

Keep in mind that each of these emerges with one of two primary motives: to influence relationships or to impede vision. I'll begin with the relational faces and conclude with the latter.

Fear of Missing Out/Comparison

Fear will very often present itself as the inner tension of missing out. We alluded to this earlier in the chapter, but it's the garden temptation in all of us to think that if we're not there, doing this, acquiring this, or showing up like this, then something in our life is lacking. This is exacerbated by our constant exposure to others' lives through social platforms and digital outlets. And the struggle of scrolling sends us on spirals of fear-based decisions.

Comparison remains the thief of all joy. This has been proven true as our culture constantly pursues more and we still find ourselves unfulfilled at each destination. Acquisition still leaves us unsettled. Affirmation still leaves us empty. J. Cole had a song on his 2014 hit album *2014 Forest Hills Drive* called "Love Yourz." In it, he advocates for learning to appreciate what presently exists within one's life, with a hook that goes, "There's no such thing as a life that is better than yours . . . and you ain't never gonna be happy 'til you love yours."[1]

The apostle Paul gives us an antidote for this face of fear by encouraging us in his letter to the church of Philippi. He reminds us to ask God for all we need but also thank him for all he has done (Phil. 4:6). We must hold our pursuits and our gratitude in tension to overcome the fear of comparison. Thanksgiving helps us value our present and gives us fuel for the future.

False Humility

Humility is one of the lost treasures of our society. Those who need it rarely have it. But we also are facing another cultural complex: Those who have it almost have too much of it. Now, that may sound strange, but have you ever met someone who went to great lengths to diminish their accomplishments and abilities?

It's almost as if we're so afraid to be seen as conceited that we think it's noble to present ourselves as common on every level. God forbid we're proud of our successes. Or that we actually have something of value to share with others because of the knowledge we've gained through hard work and experience. This inner tension causes us to fearfully engage with the world around us, dimming a light that should be shining bright.

Humility is not thinking less of yourself, it's thinking of yourself less. It's the ability to leverage your wisdom, influence, experiences, and accomplishments for the good of those you're connected to or called to serve. If we're not careful, fear will compromise our true character, dim our light, and cause us to speak small of ourselves. Sometimes we have to catch our comments and say, "That's not me talking; that sounds like fear."

Calling Committees

One of the ways fear shows its ugly head is when we rely too much on the voices of others. I like to call this "calling committees"—gathering other voices and opinions before we can feel confident to stand by our own decisions.

If you've ever watched any depiction of White House drama or action, there's usually a scene in the Situation Room. This is a room where the president of the United States gathers representatives from various branches of leadership to advise on how to handle situations in times of war or crisis. The truth is we all have a Situation Room, and if we're not careful, we'll allow fear to make us believe that every decision, act of obedience, or next step requires a committee conversation before action.

Please don't misunderstand me. I believe in the proverb that says there is wisdom in a multitude of counsel. However, we must be careful not to allow our need for counsel to become an unhealthy need for affirmation. Sometimes fear exposes itself when we can't make any choices without the convening of a committee. For your next decision, you may not need a vote; you just need vision.

Isolation

Fear often shows up in acts of isolation. Any time we are failing to engage socially and living absent of community, we may want to ask, "Is this a comfort or a fear?" Comfort says I need a break; fear says I need a barrier. Comfort says I need to recharge; fear says I need to reject.

In Ecclesiastes 4:9–12, King Solomon tells us that two is better than one, and three is even better. He goes on to give us metaphors such as two soldiers fighting back-to-back in protection of each other or a rope that is braided, producing strength and resilience. In both illustrations, his advocacy is for us to have both vision and value for what community provides in our life.

However, when fear shows up, it masks itself in things like offense and insecurity or sometimes as personality or preference, so much so that we choose isolation over intimacy. Loneliness over life with others. Safety over the necessary risk that relationships bring. But this is very often the fruit of fear. And when fear drives, it never takes us toward people; it takes us away from them.

Each of the aforementioned fears compromises the quality of our relationships. They dilute our ability to show up fully as ourselves or to show up at all. They cause us to depend too much on the opinions of the crowd over the call of our life and bring out the worst versions of ourselves.

The next four faces of fear generally show up as an impediment to vision. Let's take a look.

Procrastination

This may be the most prominent face of fear as it relates to vision. Often, our delay is not due to network, ability, or access but simply to procrastination. We put off pursuing our purpose for months or even years. Inherently, we know there's never a perfect time or an ideal season to bring a vision to life. Yet, our delayed progress is underscored by excuses and escapes of every kind.

Ultimately, procrastination is the arrogance to believe that opportunity will always be waiting and that it's God's obligation to provide it in every season. When we operate our lives from this place, we make time and opportunity unlimited resources, not seasonal offerings. But it is the latter that is the truth.

In Ecclesiastes 3, we find words about time and seasons. They are a picture-perfect display of our human experience:

> For everything there is a season,
>   a time for every activity under heaven.
> A time to be born and a time to die.
>   A time to plant and a time to harvest.
> A time to kill and a time to heal.
>   A time to tear down and a time to build up.
> A time to cry and a time to laugh.
>   A time to grieve and a time to dance.
> A time to scatter stones and a time to gather stones.
>   A time to embrace and a time to turn away.
> A time to search and a time to quit searching.
>   A time to keep and a time to throw away.
> A time to tear and a time to mend.
>   A time to be quiet and a time to speak.

> A time to love and a time to hate.
> A time for war and a time for peace. (vv. 1–8 NLT)

The theme that Solomon is outlining is clear. Timing reflects a limited opportunity. Seasons will change, opportunities will evolve, and moments will move. Learning how to maximize opportunities is vital to the person who wants more out of life but has allowed procrastination to be their default setting.

Fact-Finding

Fear is not always rooted in a lie; sometimes it's laced with truth. When facts become your only filter, you leave no room for faith-based decisions. This particular face of fear is easiest to justify. Why? Because it's using proven information.

My high school sweetheart and now wife is an auditor. This means that Excel spreadsheets, formulas, and measurable data are her love language. Throughout our relationship I have had to learn how to develop a greater appreciation for the facts. And yet, a value for them doesn't mean I'm dominated by them. The facts are there to provide insights, not to dilute inspiration.

Let me caution you: Fear will sometimes send you on a fishing expedition for an abundance of facts. And while there is wisdom in being informed, if your need for the facts becomes an impediment to forward progress, you may be seeing a face of fear. Don't be scared of facts. But don't submit to them either.

Fact-finding does not have to be fact-binding. Allow facts to be a bridge to innovation, not a barrier to inspiration. Allow facts to tell you the risk but not the route. Stay inspired, stay focused, stay faithful to moving forward.

Exaggeration

Have you ever known someone who exaggerated the stories they told? Those people in your life who require you to interpret or investigate the accuracy of the details they share because embellishment is their go-to communication method? This is not a moment of judgment, as I truly believe we have a great need for these amazing storytellers in our life.

However, we must take a careful look in the mirror, as exaggeration can become a mask we wear to polish our egos. The true danger in this practice is that it erodes the confidence our listeners have in us and has the opposite consequence: What we seek to add value to our vision actually compromises it.

Fear can often use this face when it's challenging our insecurities. It will whisper in our ears, telling us that if we don't add to the numbers, data, or message, then it's not enough. Worse yet, *we're* not enough. But our pushback has to be our confidence that the truth is enough to bring our vision to life.

Overcommitment

Have you ever made a "yes-mess"? A friend asks if you're available, and your default response is to confirm you are. However, as the days draw nearer to the event or outing or project, you start asking yourself what made you say yes. Maybe it was fear of letting people down or fear of being seen as unsupportive. We can say yes with our mouth before our mind has weighed the cost.

Ultimately, our commitments shape our life, each one defining us in some way or another. How do you know it's a commitment? If it requires time, energy, resources, attention, and sacrifice, it's likely a commitment of sorts or stems from one. And commitments can come in all shapes and sizes.

Buying a home or a car is a commitment. Getting married is a commitment. Choosing a school to pursue your education is a commitment. Having children is a commitment. Selecting a church is a commitment. Choosing a career or a company to further that career is a commitment. Establishing a relationship of any kind, whether friendship, mentorship, or sponsorship, is a commitment. And these commitments shape the very fabric of our lives and the legacies we will someday leave.

Overcommitment is a way fear masks itself. We can live with rhythm and healthy priorities, but fear will tell us that saying no will ruin our future opportunities. Or even worse, it can turn out that what people get from our gifts is below our potential because our overcommitment is causing underperformance. Unmask the fear and reframe your commitments. This is a freer and fuller life indeed.

Each of these faces presents as innocent, casual, and unassuming. And yet their mere presence can be an indication of fear lurking in the shadows of our story. If left unaddressed, their footprints will track insecurities, deceit, and fear-based decisions through the home of our hearts.

So, what do we do to live a life free from the faces of fear? Here are three simple practices to manage it.

Practice 1: Devotion

Psalm 63:1 states, "You are my God; Early will I seek You" (NKJV). I think not only the practice but the priority is important here. Devotion is not a response to our day but a preparation for what it holds. When we take on seasons without fuel for the engine, fire for the soul, we are bound to find ourselves running on empty.

Consistency in devotion is not just a way to face our fears but a way to find them lurking in our life. Our ability to discern and gain clarity on what face of fear may be in front of us is vital to our daily success.

Last, we don't simply devote time to God; we defend time with him. This daily time of surrender must be covered by our rhythms and habits. The consequence of not doing so is to allow faces to turn into masks. Masks to turn into identities. And fear to run free in our story. But with daily devotion, we peel back the layers of fear to find our true selves and futures.

Practice 2: Detection

Discovering the faces of fear may be the most important practice of our daily lives. Very often, fear's face goes undetected, leaving a series of unnecessary disappointments and detours along the way. In devotion, we can't just have the desire to discover fear in our lives but must also have the strategies that will support this discovery.

In moments such as these, I have found Psalm 139 to be not only a good passage for reflection but a formula for detection. Let's go through two verses from this chapter together to see this practice at work.

> Search me, O God, and know my heart;
>   test me and know my anxious thoughts.
> Point out anything in me that offends you,
>   and lead me along the path of everlasting life.
>   (vv. 23–24 NLT)

Search me, know my heart: This invitation allows for inspection of both our public display and our internal disposition. See what I say but also what I feel. See what I communicate but also what I carry. See what I share but also what I hide. Search my heart, for it is there that my truth fully resides.

Test me, know my anxious thoughts: This is an invitation to be stretched, tested, and refined. Refining is not a passive process but an active and aggressive one. To confirm an object's readiness for use, it often endures a stress test.

Point out anything in me that offends you: Help me discover how my decisions, habits, and practices are honoring my purpose and relationship of priority. Help me see where I've become distracted or have succumbed to the disguise of fear in my life.

Lead me along the path of everlasting life: May my next decisions and directions be the by-product of pure and righteous sources. May I be led by faith more than fear, by obedience more than opinions.

Practice 3: Discipline

Ultimately, our ability to sustain these practices will help us stay aware and active in the fight against fear. It has often been said that successful people do consistently what average people do occasionally. Our commitment is what defines our character and our future.

In Hebrews 12:11, we find the words, "No discipline seems pleasant at the time, but painful. Later on, however, it produces a harvest of righteousness and peace for those who have been trained by it."

Let's sign up to be trained by discipline. The art of being searched, tested, and exposed for our own good. It's in this internal pursuit that we can better discover just what is in the driver's seat of our lives. Even more, we can place our faith and hope at the wheel.

Fear has many faces. But today we unveil them so that our lives and our futures can be found. We lay down the masks that have long shown up in our relationships and pursuits, and say, "I am enough, as I am called by God, and in his will and presence I'll find all I need."

Take a look in the mirror. Smile back at yourself. That's more like it. This person, mask-free, is who you forever want to be.

THREE

The Breakup

It's not you, it's me.

Whether you've heard these words or said these words, you know exactly what they mean. Whatever was between us is coming to an end. It was good while it lasted, but it is no more.

If you've ever experienced a breakup, you know it's rarely easy. We often replay moments and conversations and consider both actions expressed and actions allowed. If it comes as a surprise, we ask ourselves questions like, *What did I miss?* Breakups just plain ole hurt.

As you know by now, Ashley and I were high school sweethearts. We met in our sophomore year of high school and dated throughout our teenage years. When many people hear our story, in terms of time, what they hear is that we met at sixteen and we've been together for twenty years.

However, there's a little more to our story. You see, as we went to college, distractions, difficulties, and disappointments were a part of our regular rhythm. And there was an emerging term at the time that was reserved for people like us—those who wanted the freedom to consider other options but also maintain connection to what was to remain an ongoing opportunity.

In dating, we don't call this a *breakup*; we call this a *break*. Almost every fall semester, Ashley and I would be on a break.

For those new to this vocabulary, let me attempt to culturally define it:

A temporary suspension from commitment

An evaluation period by which both parties can consider returning to exclusivity at any time

A short-term exploration period intentionally left ambiguous so either party can have plausible deniability about infractions during the period of the break

Now, for those of you who got excited and potentially think I'm advocating for this, let me get to my point before I lose you. Breaks are unwise. They do the three worst things you can do to a relationship: leave you unclear, uncommitted, and uncovered.

Even worse, they are an open door to a repetitive cycle—a way of saying we can always try this again if it's convenient. The problem is that marriage isn't about convenience. Parenting isn't about convenience. Entrepreneurship isn't about convenience. Leadership isn't about convenience. These are roles marked by commitment when they're at their best.

Why does this matter in a book about facing our fears? Because fear, at its core, is a relationship above all else. Fear is more attached to your feelings than to any other part of your being.

And as we all know, relationships are easy to start and hard to end. Fear is betting on you taking a break but returning to the routine in due time. It's willing to allow a temporary suspension from your insecurities as long as you pick them back up when triggered. It's open to you listening to speeches, podcasts, sermons, and songs that encourage you to have faith, as long as you continue answering the calls and being available for conversation.

The heart of this book is the hope that you would divorce the patterns that keep you from fully breaking up with fear. That you would embrace the life that is waiting for you on the other side of this toxic relationship.

That you would actually realize that it is you. That fear is not even to blame. Are you ready to hear the hard truth? For many of us, we are the problem. It's not fear, it's me. Me who keeps the door open to mediocrity, insecurity, settling, and procrastination. Me who continues to wear the faces of fear. Me who chooses to stay in something that only hurts or hinders my future. That's on me.

Ultimately, fear is a parasite. That is its only power. A parasite is an organism that lives in or on another species, its host, and benefits by deriving nutrients at the other's expense.

Fear cannot live on its own; it is fed by parts of us that we know exist but often leave unaddressed. Today we take accountability. But accountability starts with awareness.

Just before we jump into these three areas where fear feeds, I think it's important that we know this is not always about sin, and that fear is what I like to call a weight. I think this is what the writer of the book of Hebrews was saying when they penned the words found in Hebrews 12:1. Here are a few different translations for us to consider as we grapple with this caution:

> Therefore we also, since we are surrounded by so great a cloud of witnesses, let us lay aside every weight, and the sin which so easily ensnares us, and let us run with endurance the race that is set before us. (NKJV)

> Therefore, since we are surrounded by such a great cloud of witnesses, let us throw off everything that hinders and the sin that so easily entangles. And let us run with perseverance the race marked out for us. (NIV)

> Such a large crowd of witnesses is all around us! So we must get rid of everything that slows us down, especially the sin that just won't let go. And we must be determined to run the race that is ahead of us. (CEV)

> Do you see what this means—all these pioneers who blazed the way, all these veterans cheering us on? It means we'd better get on with it. Strip down, start running—and never quit! No extra spiritual fat, no parasitic sins. (MSG)

Did you see that last one? Parasitic sins. But there is a dual description here. This isn't about just addressing sin but also addressing weights, entanglements, hindrances, and other things that slow us down. From what? Purpose, potential, power, possibility. The best version of you is a lighter version, a faster version, a freer version, a version cleansed of parasitic attachments.

Parasites depend on their host to feed them and keep them alive. The same goes for our fears. There are things we do or believe that constantly feed our fears and keep them growing in and hindering our lives. Let's look at some of the "food sources" of our fears.

Fear Feeds on Familiarity

This will come up several times throughout this work because familiarity is one of the sneakiest ways fear creeps into our story. We don't notice it because the conversation, individual, or habit has always been there. Actually, it feels stranger when it's not present than when it is. This is often the origin of cycles.

We don't repeat cycles because we like the results; we repeat cycles because we only know our routine. Life beyond the routine is actually what's foreign. And this is why we tend to return to what's known versus what's new.

This cyclical reality allows fear to walk into our lives unannounced quite often. It plays on the comfort we have and dwells in those comfortable environments. Very often, we don't even recognize its return until a triggering event reveals its existence.

Fear Feeds on Facts

Do you know what can kill the vibes at a cookout? Mosquitoes. I have seen that little insect clear out an event quicker than a physical fight. When people have had enough of them, they'll usually say something like, "They are eating me up." However, that's not all the way accurate.

What generally occurs is the drinking of our blood. It's definitely giving Dracula for a moment here. Only female mosquitoes bite humans, and they do it to get what entomologists call a "blood meal." This allows them to derive proteins from our blood to produce their eggs. But that's not all. While not as common, they also can be responsible for leaving something behind. As you may know, mosquitoes can carry viruses and infections, and those can be life-threatening in some cases.

Fear operates in a very similar way. Sometimes it's there to take. Other times, it's there to plant. But you can't ignore it in either case.

Fear needs something from you in familiarity, but when it comes to facts, it also wants to leave something in you. In your head, in your heart, in your habits. Facts are neutral; they are neither good nor bad, but they are defined by the circumstances that shape them.

This means fear doesn't need the facts until you're considering moving forward on a dream or an idea. Then what was sown in your head or heart comes to the surface. You find out in that moment that fear was feeding on the facts of your past, and those thoughts are impeding your initiative. Generally, when you decide to publicize your business venture, the "fear facts" of failed attempts emerge in your psyche. Or "fear facts" emerge when you start writing the book but then you hear that inner voice say, "This is not a new attempt, and you've never finished before, so why would you finish now?" Fear can lie dormant in facts, but never forget that history is not a destination. So, while we learn from the past, we don't run toward it.

Fear Feeds on Fatigue

The worst version of me is the tired version of me. The same may be true for you too. Exhaustion often works against our ability to maintain resolve, clarity, and consistency. And fear feeds on our fatigue. When we're tired, we may be more likely to cut corners. We may be more likely to compromise our character.

This is why rhythms of rest are essential to set and protect. We see examples of this throughout Scripture. It's probably not an accident that the command to "remember the Sabbath day by keeping it holy" listed in the Ten Commandments along with its detailed explanation is the longest one given (Exod. 20:8). Or when we look at the life of Jesus, we regularly see him go to a quiet, secluded place away from crowds to be alone. Mark 1:35 tells us, "Very early in the morning, while it was still dark, Jesus got up, left the house and went off to a solitary place, where he prayed." Or, in Matthew 14:23: "After he had dismissed them, he went up on a mountainside by himself to pray. Later that night, he was there alone." It would seem that Jesus wasn't intimidated by the quiet nor afflicted by being alone. These rhythms give us time not just to rest but also to reset and operate at an optimal level.

Fear, however, thrives on our hurry. Busyness has become a badge of honor for so many in our society. But hurry is the great enemy of the soul.

As Dallas Willard is known to have said, we must "ruthlessly eliminate hurry from our lives." He saw this as a tool of the tempter to compromise our fullness of life. If this is true, that means fear is able to find fulfillment in our fatigue. To push against this temptation is a symbol of resistance. Rest is a holy rebellion against a fatigued world.

■ ■ ■

In the '80s and '90s, I like to think sitcoms were in their prime. These were the days before watching on demand, streaming, or rewinding your TV were available. You couldn't miss the time slot, and families would eagerly await shows coming on, gather around the one TV in the family room, and laugh and follow the storylines together.

In 1989, a classic sitcom called *Family Matters* emerged, capturing the hearts of many families all over the country. The featured characters were the Winslows, an African American family navigating the day-to-day realities of life, love, and family. And central to the story was their next-door neighbor, Steve Urkel, a bona fide nerd full of intellect and unintentional humor, who had a huge crush on the Winslows' daughter Laura.

At one point in the show's timeline, Steve invents a machine that allows him to transform. He steps in as Steve Urkel and steps out as Stefan. Stefan was a teenage heartthrob. Tall, stylish, popular, fit, and charismatic. I could go on and on about episodes of *Family Matters*, but here's the point.

Wouldn't it be nice if we could all transform just as easily? I mean, step into a machine with our fears and step out without them. Step in with our fatigue and step out energized. Step in with our scars and step out totally healed and whole.

Unfortunately, that machine hasn't been invented just yet. Which means our transformation is often a process of intentionality and intimacy with God. In Scripture, I think the transformation I find to be most intriguing is that of Gideon.

When we meet Gideon, he is threshing wheat in a winepress to hide it from enemy soldiers. Translation: He is hiding something from his community's bully because his people have no intention of standing up for themselves at all.

Then, when Gideon least expects it, while doing the thing that defines him as being afraid, God speaks to him. Here's the exchange:

> The angel of the LORD came and sat down under the oak in Ophrah that belonged to Joash the Abiezrite, where his son Gideon was threshing wheat in a winepress to keep it from

the Midianites. When the angel of the LORD appeared to Gideon, he said, "The LORD is with you, mighty warrior."

"Pardon me, my lord," Gideon replied, "but if the LORD is with us, why has all this happened to us? Where are all his wonders that our ancestors told us about when they said, 'Did not the LORD bring us up out of Egypt?' But now the LORD has abandoned us and given us into the hand of Midian."

The LORD turned to him and said, "Go in the strength you have and save Israel out of Midian's hand. Am I not sending you?"

"Pardon me, my lord," Gideon replied, "but how can I save Israel? My clan is the weakest in Manasseh, and I am the least in my family."

The LORD answered, "I will be with you, and you will strike down all the Midianites, leaving none alive." (Judg. 6:11–16)

Notice how Gideon sees himself as he talks to God. "How can I do this? The family I come from has not prepared me for something like this. And I am the least of all those in my family." Gideon is full of fear, and his fear is feeding off of familiarity, facts, and fatigue.

Now, I want you to see where Gideon ends up. Let's fast-forward in the story a bit:

Dividing the three hundred men into three companies, he placed trumpets and empty jars in the hands of all of them, with torches inside.

"Watch me," he told them. "Follow my lead. When I get to the edge of the camp, do exactly as I do. When I and all who are with me blow our trumpets, then from all around the camp blow yours and shout, 'For the LORD and for Gideon.'" (Judg. 7:16–18)

This is the same Gideon. He has now assumed leadership of not just his tribe but the entire community and has led them to the brink of war against the very Midianites he was found hiding from a chapter before. And he tells them, "watch me," "follow my lead," and to "shout 'for the LORD and for Gideon.'"

Okay, I know what you're thinking. There was a transformation machine back then. He stepped in and stepped out a chapter later, fearless. That's one theory for sure. However, I'd like to propose that by following Gideon's in-between, we may find a different reasoning for how this transformation from fearful to fearless took place.

Gideon breaks up with the unhealthy relationship he has with fear, and maybe, just maybe, we'll find in his story the courage to break up with our fear as well.

Step 1: Look for the Signs

Immediately following his initial exchange with the angel of the Lord, Gideon does something important and often underutilized in the life of those facing fear. He asks God for a sign. Gideon says, "If now I have found favor in your eyes, give me a sign that it is really you talking to me. Please do not go away until I come back and bring my offering and set it before you" (Judg. 6:17–18). And what does God say? "I will wait until you return" (v. 18).

God waits on Gideon. This is so powerful and contrasts so much of our theology about faith. Gideon is full of fear, self-doubt, and in need of confirmation. So, God agrees to be patient with him. Not only that, but if you read from verse 17 until the end of the chapter, you'll find four signs in total that Gideon requests from God to confirm his call. By the end of the chapter, Gideon has made so many asks he's afraid God is going to be angry. "Then Gideon said to God, 'Do not be angry with me. Let me make just one more request.

Allow me one more test with the fleece, but this time make the fleece dry and let the ground be covered with dew.' That night God did so. Only the fleece was dry; all the ground was covered with dew" (vv. 39–40). All of chapter 6 is God meeting Gideon in the place of his insecurity and being patient with him. And he'll do the same for you.

In particular, there are three types of signs we want to be versed in. The danger in asking for a sign before learning how to recognize them is that if God gives us one but we can notice only one type, we could feel unconfirmed when God has been clear all along.

> **Sign 1: Confirmation from people.** Sometimes you will receive confirmation through people. Maybe they engage you in a conversation unexpectedly about the thing you've been praying for. Or in some instances, they may feel led to ask you if you've been praying about a particular topic. Certainly the most obvious of these is a prophetic gesture where one equipped with that gift confirms that they've heard from the Lord for you. But just keep your ears and heart open because sometimes the sign is other people.
>
> **Sign 2: Confirmation from place.** The second type of confirmation can come from a specific location. A friend of mine did a yearlong missionary journey several years ago. This was not an in-and-out commitment. Rather, he had to leave behind his jobs and life here in the States, committing to almost one year of living in different countries and submerging himself in those cultures. A part of the missional focus of their organization was not simply to go and do for these countries but also to enable American Christians to

experience the depth of discipleship happening in other parts of the world.

He told me of a morning practice in one of the countries where, for the first hour of the day, he had to meditate in silence and record any specific images, locations, or visions that emerged. He mentioned that for the first week or so it felt pointless and idealistic. However, he said that by the third week, as he became clearer, slower, and more full of faith, he started to see places and specific locations he had never visited. Then he said something I didn't expect: Very often, without planning to, throughout a given day he would be standing in or bump into those locations that he'd envisioned that morning.

Now, maybe you think that's impossible. I'm simply saying that whether you meditate for an hour or just feel like a location gives you goosebumps, pay attention to the signs that places provide.

Sign 3: Confirmation from prompting. Some confirmation will be felt on the inside. Promptings may be experienced as an inner nudge or push to do or say something. It could also be felt as an inner tug to pull back and not do or say something. Prompting is an active way the Holy Spirit gets our attention and calls us to the will of God.

The first thing Gideon does is ask for a sign before he takes the next step. So, what's step number two?

Step 2: Trust the Small Instructions

I've come to find that faith doesn't just ask for one big decision but invites you to several small decisions on the way.

This was true for Gideon. There were small opportunities to build trust and work the muscle of faith prior to the central battle. This is where we find Gideon in Judges 7:

> The LORD said to Gideon, "You have too many men. I cannot deliver Midian into their hands, or Israel would boast against me, 'My own strength has saved me.' Now announce to the army, 'Anyone who trembles with fear may turn back and leave Mount Gilead.'" So twenty-two thousand men left, while ten thousand remained.
>
> But the LORD said to Gideon, "There are still too many men. Take them down to the water, and I will thin them out for you there. If I say, 'This one shall go with you,' he shall go; but if I say, 'This one shall not go with you,' he shall not go."
>
> So Gideon took the men down to the water. There the LORD told him, "Separate those who lap the water with their tongues as a dog laps from those who kneel down to drink." Three hundred of them drank from cupped hands, lapping like dogs. All the rest got down on their knees to drink.
>
> The LORD said to Gideon, "With the three hundred men that lapped I will save you and give the Midianites into your hands. Let all the others go home." (vv. 2–7)

Gideon starts with thirty-two thousand men and ends up with three hundred. This is what I like to call a trust-builder moment. It's not the original assignment that God called him to, but it's a stepping stone to build his faith before he gets there.

Notice that even this moment is packaged in several steps. His dependence on the many fighters is used to refine his confidence in the more reliable source. Wherever there is a reduction, it's usually an invitation to the revelation that all you need is God.

Each phase of decrease is an opportunity for Gideon's faith to increase. You could see fewer men as more fear or more faith. But all of this is serving the transformation of Gideon from coward to courageous, worrier to warrior.

Finally, we arrive at step three, which takes place right on the brink of battle. They can literally see the enemy's camp from where they are positioned.

Step 3: Do It Scared

What I love about Gideon's story is that it's not devoid of humanity. After all that, he still has some fear left in him. This is the reminder that the goal is not to become fearless, per se, but to fear less. Look at what God says to Gideon: "Get up, go down against the camp, because I am going to give it into your hands. If you are afraid to attack, go down to the camp with your servant Purah and listen to what they are saying. Afterward, you will be encouraged to attack the camp" (Judg. 7:9–11).

Don't miss the start of verse 10: "If you are afraid." God doesn't say he won't use you. Or that he's tired of having this conversation with you. He says you can attack now, but if you're afraid, he'll still give you more signs and more instruction and more support to increase your faith.

I love how this moment with God is so affirming and involves action items. He doesn't invite Gideon to a kumbaya session. He says to do something and hear something. Activity is always the posture God responds to most. Even scared, do it.

By the time Gideon transforms into this confident and bold leader, we see a verse later that fear was still present. And yet fear didn't disqualify him. He did it scared, and God was with him. You can do it scared, too, and he'll be with you.

Now, before I conclude this chapter, I want to share with you something that's sobering but central to your theology. Just because you faced a fear doesn't mean it's not a fear that follows you. Just because you broke up with it doesn't mean it broke up with you. It's for this reason that you must remain connected to God's voice and heart so that you stay alert and aware of fear's desire to creep back into your life.

It's time to break up with fear and find the version of you that's ready for more. More life, more freedom, more faith. Look for the signs, trust the small instructions, and do it scared.

No more excuses, no more waiting. Call it what it is and leave it where it is. We're not on a break, we're moving on. It's not you, it's me. I'm different. I'm ready. I'm free.

FOUR

Fear Is Not Hard to Find

Are you afraid of the dark?

This is a judgment-free zone if you are. I believe that nightlights may not scare away monsters, but they definitely protect from stubbed toes in the dark. And let's face it, there's nothing that challenges your spirituality like a stubbed toe. But seriously, beyond the literal question, when I hear those words, I find myself reflecting on a certain show from the '90s. If you're unfamiliar, let me catch you up.

Are You Afraid of the Dark? was a show that aired weekly on Nickelodeon. Each episode began with a group of teenagers who represented what was known as the Midnight Society. They'd gather around their meeting spot at the fire, and one of the teens would be identified as the storyteller. After beginning the story, the episode would tell the tale of horror firsthand.

As I reflected on that show, I couldn't help but think that there are similar episodes for us as a world. Fear is fueling our politics, our social lives, our parenting, even our religious practices. And it's filling our children. They no longer have to meet at a campfire to share their horrors. The steady stream of horror stories lies at their fingertips all day long. From social media timelines to news headlines, fear is not hard to find.

This fear-consuming paradigm is relatively new to our culture. I remember a time when we used to roam the neighborhood until the streetlights came on. The bus-stop bully was a necessary part of your coming-of-age journey. The first dance was a welcome anxiety as you wondered, *Do I go Michael Jackson moves first or a relaxed two-step?* These were normal anxieties considered par for the course.

Unfortunately, those days feel long gone. We've traded neighborhood support for community skepticism. We don't encourage our kids to face bullies; we tell them to avoid them because fights no longer are fought fair. We model "Stay away" much better than we model "Get to know." All of this is driven by a human departure from embracing the fears that used to form us and instead avoiding them altogether.

This is not without good reason. As we consume more media made with fear as its base ingredient, we are feeling the weight of that reality. Mental health professionals are developing new language to define these trends. Phrases like "doomscrolling," "headline anxiety," and "headline stress disorder" are all attempts to define the effects of fear-based messaging delivered through the vehicles of clickbait and headlines.

Now, in order to face it, we must understand it.

So, what is fear? It is widely recognized as a primal emotion in response to a real danger or perceived threat. It is innate in all of us to experience it. To be human is to know fear. Here are a few things we should know about fear itself.

Fear is physical. It alters your body in many ways. Your blood pressure and heart rate go up. Your nervous system begins to adjust to the circumstances. Your body begins preparing for what we know to be the fight-or-flight response. All of these physical responses are triggered by the presence of fear.

For many, fear shows up in our bodies before it shows up in our actions. These reactions tell us a great deal about the environments and interactions that impact us most.

Fear is personal. It is not universal. Our own individual experiences, history, environmental exposure, and wiring all inform how we respond to fear. There is not a one-size-fits-all approach.

Learning how to both identify and communicate our personal fears is vital to our lived experience. Fear should never be dismissed or assumed, as it takes on many forms in many different lives.

Fear is necessary. Fear is natural and informs us of dangers and threats. These primal cautions are actually there to protect us from circumstances that could compromise our health.

Without fear, we would be less human, less protected, and less responsible. A huge part of maturation is the acknowledgment of fear without bowing to it. It teaches us, reminds us, and protects us.

The presence of fear is not the problem. Not yielding control to it is what we're after in this book. We want to ensure that we have not forfeited control to but rather have a healthy relationship with the natural experiences and emotions that will emerge in life.

Fear is inevitable, faith is intentional, and our future is determined by how we manage both in concert with each other.

In a 2023 study by Chapman University, they surveyed Americans' fears.[1] Here were the top ten fears of 2023 per their research:

1. Corrupt government officials
2. Economic/financial collapse
3. Russia using nuclear weapons
4. The US becoming involved in another world war
5. People I love becoming seriously ill
6. People I love dying
7. Pollution of drinking water
8. Biological warfare
9. Cyberterrorism
10. Not having enough money for the future

This survey became the catalyst for a book called *Fear Itself*, in which the researchers outlined the top one hundred fears.[2] If you're like my wife and you watch *Law & Order: SVU* religiously, then you're wondering where "murder by a stranger" is—that's number 50. Break-ins is number 38. Heights is number 41, and animals are in the 90s. Fear is very broad and open to interpretation.

What is clear is that all of our fears fall into three categories. Each category represents a unique stressor in our life that we must steward. They each carry their own unique threat and require a unique strategy to successfully overcome them.

Category 1: Personal Fears

Personal fears are those that affect us uniquely. Even if they are common aspects of life, the experience we have with them affects our quality of life. The appropriate response to personal fears must be customization over comparison. Attempting to craft a universal response to a personal reality is not only ineffective but often unsustainable. By nature, what makes fears personal is the fact that while they might be common, they can affect each of us differently.

Fear is naturally a perennial topic for discussions and polls. Now, if you're a millennial in America, this makes sense for some of us. We've lived through more mass shootings than any previous generation. Consequently, for some there is an assumption that preceding generations may not have carried fears the same way.

This also presents in less traumatic—but no less personal—ways. The fears of animals, heights, clowns, roller coasters, or needles all represent various personal fears we might carry through life.

Why are personal fears so easy to embrace? Usually because of shame. Shame is the trait in all of us that reasons that if we share our full selves, then we'll be seen differently. Or even worse, treated differently. This then prompts us to lie, become avoidant, or isolate in hopes of experiencing freedom from the pain that exposure produces.

The best response to personal fears is verbalizing your fears. Sharing your fears with a trusted friend or through talk therapy, when more professional help is needed, is vital to your emotional well-being. It's also healthy to organize your fears by intensity. Knowing which fears have a greater impact on your day-to-day life will not only help you articulate the support you need from others but will also help you build a strategy for your personal engagement with others.

Category 2: Social/Communal Fears

In the book *Fear Itself*, one of the central findings was that most fears reflect social constructs and exposure. For example, if you were raised in a home that was highly committed to politics, you are likely to carry fears related to government. If you were raised in a neighborhood where over-policing took place, you are likely to have more fears related to law enforcement engagement.

If you are Black in America, your list looks very different from those of your White counterparts. If you're a boomer, you are likely to carry very different fears than Generation Z. Why? Because our lived experience, history, conversations, and community all inform what we deem are credible fears. If you are from a community that had low crime, both your lack of experience with crime and the potential absence of a narrative around it affect how much you worry about the possibility of crime occurring.

It's important to note that this is not to validate these fears. Rather, this is to elevate the data that confirms whether they were personal fears or inherited as a result of the environments we were influenced by.

Social fear is what drives us to carry disgust at political "others" or to judge some fears more harshly than others.

Why are social fears so easy to embrace? Simply put, because of confirmation bias and norms. There has never been a time in human history when it's been easier to find validation for your position. Consequently, if I'm afraid, whether the fear is legitimate or not, I can find one hundred articles about people who agree with my concern.

The best response to social and communal fears is to seek diverse relationships beyond your normal groups. Pursue material and research that broadens your firmly held beliefs. Finally, this is a great place to foster risk-taking in your life. Don't assume that the fear that you carry is confirmed by the masses just because it was confirmed by your community.

Category 3: Existential Fears

Existential fears are related to our existence, purpose, and perceived value on the earth. These are often hardest to communicate because they relate to how we worry about our existence and legacy in life. Questions that emerge when we're grappling with existential fears could sound like:

> What is my purpose?
> Who am I without that job or position?
> What if I can't provide for my family?
> What if I am a failure?
> Is my life making a difference at all?

These fears are often rooted in our deeply held ideas about ourselves. They demand us to consider our goodness, our worth, our value, and our purpose in the world. Even if they are inconsistent with our reality, they present themselves as legitimate and are hard to answer. As a consequence, they can often become forces driving us to overwork or withdraw altogether.

Why are existential fears so easy to embrace? Because they are easily masked. We can smile over them, we can post in contradiction to them, we can engage socially without ever revealing them. Consequently, we can be eroding internally under the weight of these concerns, but no one ever knows it until the fear has eaten away at our core.

The best response to existential fears is to establish a pre-selected group where vulnerability is shared. A place where you not only feel empowered to share but you can hear the fears and inner wrestlings of others as well. These safe spaces can become an oasis for your soul—not always for answers but for understanding.

Whether you locate personal fears, social fears, or existential fears, they can't be ignored; they must be faced. When we live worry-filled, we also live worry-fueled, which impacts our relationships, rhythms, and reality.

Unfortunately, fear alone is not impacting our world. Our fears are compounded by an additional threat to us finding freedom: anxiety.

Anxiety is similar to fear, but they are not the same. The Diagnostic and Statistical Manual of Mental Disorders (DSM) defines *fear* as "the emotional response to real or perceived threat," whereas *anxiety* is defined as the anticipation of a future threat.[3] Please note that both can be necessary and even healthy, but when left uncontrolled, they can become disorders. Let's look at a few stats.

In his book *The Anxious Generation*, Jonathan Haidt shares that since 2010, depression has increased 106 percent and anxiety has increased 134 percent among college students.[4]

Looking at the US population as a whole, the US National Survey on Drug Use and Health found that since 2010, anxiety has increased by 139 percent in people ages 18–25, by 103 percent in ages 26–34, and by 52 percent in ages 35–49.[5]

We are growing more fearful and more anxious, and living a life beyond fear is becoming harder. But we can push back against the tide and take control of our lives. One decision, one relationship, one day at a time.

■ ■ ■

As mentioned earlier, I'm a proud cancer survivor. Because of my age at the time of my diagnosis and the length of my treatment, I found very early in my journey the whisper of fear in my everyday life. My treatment plan specifically outlined rigorous inpatient chemotherapy treatments.

I would go into the hospital every few weeks for a three-to-five-day stay of IV-released medicines. Ifosfamide, doxorubicin, and methotrexate were my primary three. As treatment began, I started seeing the effects take hold of my body. I'd lay my head down on my pillow, and patches of my hair would remain once I lifted it back up again. My inability to hold down food due to nausea would cause me to go three or four days without eating. My strength was limited as a consequence, and my body withered away to an unrecognizable size.

I recall an early conversation our family had with the doctors, where they explained that the treatment could not be targeted to only kill the compromised cells. Rather, the treatment targets all cells equally. Which means that to kill the cancer we are also weakening aspects of the body that are unaffected.

I watched week in and week out as what was being put in my body worked to heal while simultaneously causing hurt. There were days where silent tears filled my eyes. What those tears wanted to communicate was that enough was enough, that I couldn't take it anymore, and that I wondered if it was worth it.

But I reconciled that with the fact that there was life on the other side of this. A life worth finding and living.

Fighting your fears and worries is not a sure science. I'm not here with a silver bullet. I am here with a suggestion: Become brave. Now, if that sounds like a message on the back of a cereal box, stick with me. Bravery is, at its bottom line, a series of choices. More often than not, it's not even about success.

We award medals to soldiers who showed bravery in the line of duty, not because they won an individual encounter or, in the worst instances, might have even lost their life. The award is not because they triumphed but because they tried. We reward humanitarians not because they saved everyone but because they tried. And bravery is not reserved for international accomplishment. It takes bravery as a single mother to look at your children and say, "I got you." It takes bravery to stand with those who've been silenced in your community. It takes bravery to speak out against workplace inequity. Brave living is not waiting on something; it's waiting on someone. And maybe, just maybe, that someone is you. Your voice, your life, and your story could change everything.

Likewise, a brave life is a full life. It doesn't mean that trying doesn't invite hurt and change, pain and pressure. But worry has run our lives long enough. Let's try another way.

Become Brave with People

Othering has become one of the great walls of humanity in our society. Walls of mistrust, hatred, disgust, dissension, and confusion. The higher the wall, the deeper the divide. Walls don't just keep strangers out either. They separate us from family, friends, coworkers, neighbors, and allies.

When suggesting that we should be brave with people, we must take into account that fear around relationships is at an all-time high. It is a commonly held estimation that some forty million Americans struggle with social anxiety, much of which is tied to the fear of social rejection.

What this means is that when we choose to be brave with people, we are mounting an attack on a culture of isolation and loneliness. We must decide that, yes, as scary as it may be for relationships to not work, friendships to end, or people to hurt us, our commitment to becoming brave is greater than the comfort of settling for a life of solitude.

This could look like committing to adding social acquaintances. Or joining a social group where running or some other hobby is shared. Or serving at your local church to get more involved in the communal offering of story and struggle.

As I highlighted earlier, the reality is the treatment may also cause some pain. There's no guarantee that people won't mess up in handling your vulnerability or your step into a new community. But it is guaranteed that if you don't try, you'll never experience what people can bring to your life's potential.

Become Brave with Purpose

Contrary to popular belief, purpose is not a destination but a conversation, one that is eternal in nature. Emerging versions of you are conversing with previous versions of you. We learn to love who we are becoming as we both celebrate and grieve in growth. It's brave not only to face people and pursuits around you but also to face versions of you that must be crucified for what's next.

I observed this firsthand in my marriage. In our first year of marriage, Ashley and I didn't have any children, didn't own a home, and knew everything about how to make a marriage work (insert sarcastic wink here). As you can imagine, fourteen years, two kids, two homes, and more than a few issues later, our conversations look very different now than they did then.

Why? Because marriage requires ongoing commitment to conversations that are commensurate with the shared goals and focuses of the season. Purpose is no different. Its mission might not change, but its assignment might. If you're unwilling to be flexible and develop new skills and thoughts, you'll limit just how much of your purpose you can uncover in yourself.

I believe this is why the Bible likens our relationship with God to that of a potter and clay. The potter is always aware of the final product as their hands shape, shift, and stretch the clay. If you've ever watched this process unfold, one thing is apparent: It looks messy, unpredictable, and sometimes counterproductive until the purpose emerges. While it may be a journey of curiosity for us, it was never lost on the potter what this was becoming. Purpose is a brave yes to allow the potter to mold the best version of our lives.

Become Brave with Discovery

Let's get curious about the world around us again. As a society, we've lost our heart to learn, explore, and discover the beauty of what life has to offer. We've lost our awe and wonder at what lies in front and ahead of us. We must recover the spirit of exploration and discovery.

Unfortunately, we've settled in front of televisions and screens, phones and platforms that kill our need to explore, assuming that Instagram's "Explore" page can fulfill the intrinsic need in us all to learn beyond ourselves. Almost all modern research proves that these devices we hold dearly don't get the job done. That our loss of wonder with the world has been to our own detriment.

We must regularly remind ourselves that our ability to engage in purposeful *play* is one of the healthiest motivators for work done well. Our ability to experience the world free from pressure to produce, free to experiment, fail, and find the fun in our future is vital to our vocational success.

Likewise, I believe the childlike faith in all of us must be recaptured. By doing this, we are released to discover the beauty and power of charting new courses yet again. We were once children in a world of wonder; now we are adults in a world of danger. We can't change the world until we change the way we see it. Discover what it has to offer by taking a leap of faith again.

Bravery is learning a new skill. Bravery is hiking a new mountain. Bravery is learning a new hobby. Bravery is traveling to a new country. Bravery is branching out and dating again. Bravery is stepping out and facing a fear.

Discover what life has to offer when we live beyond our fears. There's a world waiting for us to reclaim our wonder.

PART 2
BECOMING BRAVE

FIVE

Winning the War Against Worry

My wife and I planted The Life Church in the summer of 2015. It was a time of great excitement, zeal, and a lot of youthful naivete. Full of faith, we mustered up friends, mentors, college students, and grandparents to believe in this God-sized dream. We scraped together coins from every corner of our house and partnered with the generosity of others to invest in this vision that would become affectionately known as TLC. And on July 9, 2015, it all began.

We couldn't afford much, so our origin story found its roots at a local middle school in the heart of downtown Richmond. In those early days, I made the slides, set up the Behringer X32 soundboard, led praise and worship, and then preached. This particular school had wooden chairs that added to the soundtrack of Sundays just as much as the band. We had one room off the makeshift sanctuary that I used as a place to collect my thoughts. It also happened to be the janitor's closet and bathroom. Whatever picture just popped in your head, the real thing probably looked worse. And one of the most important features of the building was that there was no central air-conditioning, ensuring that summer services became an Orangetheory class just by virtue of attendance.

On multiple occasions, medical professionals in our congregation would come to me with concerns that our service posed a threat for dehydration and other heat-related illnesses. So, we'd pass out popsicles and water bottles following praise and worship. We created custom handheld fans for anyone who wanted them. And we'd rent large fans to go in the back of the auditorium that would hum their own tune, and I'd have to preach (or yell, depending on who you're asking) over them for the entirety of the sermon. Yeah, good times.

Yet, by the favor of God, the church quickly grew. Eighty people turned into two hundred. Two hundred turned into four hundred and fifty-four. I only know that number specifically due to a social media post we'd made about it in 2016 because we were so proud. Years later, hundreds have turned into thousands across multiple campuses, but it all began on that July day in the heart of a Richmond middle school.

Now, I don't share this with you for affirmation. I share it for an entirely different reason and revelation, one that may seem minor at first glance but has impacted my life greatly. What began on July 9, 2015, never stopped. It is literally still happening today, a decade later, every single weekend. You know what else didn't stop? Problems to solve. What started as concerns about the safety of parishioners overheating has evolved into many more issues over the years. Sometimes those concerns are logistical, other times emotional, many times spiritual. But the truth remains: Every single week, there's something to worry about. And it didn't take me long to realize that the emotions of starting and the emotions of sustaining are not the same.

Every Sunday, I'd get in the car following services, and for the entirety of the ride home, ramble off my worries to my wife. "How are we going to do this?" "Why did I say this?" "Do you think that person is ever coming back?" "We can't afford this, but we need it, right?" I'd like to tell you that I've completely conquered that tendency, but it still happens more often than I'd like to admit. Eventually, she gave me a time limit on how long I could wade in the waters of worry. Then I'd have to come out and work toward solutions. Sometimes, I have to learn to be okay with knowing that some of my worries will always exist.

Here's the revelation: Worry comes with it! Whatever your "it" is, you may be surprised to find that worry is riding along. TLC is no less a dream come true. Its stories, growth, and impact have been some of the greatest joys of my life. But for all its wonder, it comes with plenty to worry about.

Maybe your dream isn't starting a church.

Maybe it's starting a family.

Launching a business.

Writing or producing a project.

Sharing an idea.

Securing a promotion.

I can tell you with confidence: Worry comes with it. Children are an amazing blessing—that you will worry about from the time you learn of their existence. Leadership is an incredible responsibility—that will have you worrying about things nobody else even knows about. Added income is an admirable pursuit—that will have you worried at the end of the year, hoping you filed everything correctly.

Whatever "it" is for you, know that worry comes with it. But just because we should expect it doesn't mean we should surrender to it. In this chapter, we'll see how to win the war against worry so that we can live into the joy and freedom God has always intended for us. If you try to face fear without winning the war of worry, you'll find yourself in a cycle of disappointment. Fret not; this is a war you can win!

In Scripture, Jesus provides one of his most definitive teachings on worry during the Sermon on the Mount. In Matthew 6, in many Bibles there's a heading halfway down that says, "Do Not Worry." Following these words is Jesus's teaching on how to approach our worries.

> Therefore I tell you, do not worry about your life, what you will eat or drink; or about your body, what you will wear. Is not life more than food, and the body more than clothes? Look at the birds of the air; they do not sow or reap or store away in barns, and yet your heavenly Father feeds them. Are you not much more valuable than they? Can any one of you by worrying add a single hour to your life?
>
> And why do you worry about clothes? See how the flowers of the field grow. They do not labor or spin. Yet I tell you that not even Solomon in all his splendor was dressed like one of these. If that is how God clothes the grass of the field, which is here today and tomorrow is thrown into the fire, will he not much more clothe you—you of little faith? So do not worry, saying, "What shall we eat?" or "What shall we drink?" or "What shall we wear?" For the pagans run after all these things, and your heavenly Father knows that you need them. But seek first his kingdom and his righteousness, and all these things will be given to you as well. Therefore do not worry about tomorrow, for tomorrow will worry about itself. Each day has enough trouble of its own. (vv. 25–34)

If you've spent a good amount of time in church, you've probably come across Matthew 6:33 at some point. It's easily one of the most quoted and emphasized parts of biblical teaching. Seek first the kingdom, and everything else you need will come. However, for all that is contained in this verse's content, it's the context that we often miss. Jesus is offering this encouragement in response to his observation of how worry consumes people's lives. He witnesses their worry about things, clothes, food, achievements, and more. They worried then, and we worry now.

So, in Jesus fashion, he puts things in perspective. Matthew 6 is a prescription to help the limitations of human vision. It gives us a glimpse of how God sees our world and how he'd like us to see it as well. In particular, there are three principles in Matthew 6 that can be a battle cry for us when waging war against worry.

Principle 1: God Cares About What God Creates

Jesus observes the cares and concerns of people who are being swallowed by their own stories. He doesn't diminish the reality of their needs; he simply highlights God's track record for provision and compassion. He does this by referencing God's care for the birds of the air and the flowers of the field. His advocacy here is to get the listeners of both his time and ours to understand that God is in control of it all. Not just human life but all life.

Imagine that. God is so intentional about his creations that he ensures they have been placed in a system of supply. So birds are provided with the food they need to keep flying. Flowers are provided with the rain they need to keep growing. And we, humanity, are his prized possession. We are provided with the air we need to keep breathing. We are provided with the firing of neurons to keep us thinking. And we are provided with his best gift, the Holy Spirit, to strengthen our souls and enrich our lives. God cares about what he creates.

Jesus offers a challenge: If God does that, how much more will he do for you? God has placed us in a system of supply. He would not do for the birds of the sky, fish of the sea, and flowers of the field what he would not do for his children. Our declaration should be, "I am in a system of supply." We must hold to this affirmation in uncertain seasons if we want to win the war of worry. So, why do we fail to hold to it?

Simply put, one of worry's biggest strategies against our fortitude is the distortion of truth. Or, as I like to see it, we must win against the pressure of propaganda. Worry has a big mouth and is easy to see everywhere we look.

In World War II, war began changing in several ways. Certainly, the scale, length, and parties involved made this a defining moment in military history. However, up until this point, the primary means of conducting war were military, economic, and political. But as populations grew, as war waged longer, and as people started to challenge the political position by being more widely outspoken against war, the need for an additional element of warfare emerged—propaganda.

In *The SAGE Handbook of Propaganda*, it is acknowledged that "propaganda in wartime must seek to demoralize enemy morale. A primary objective of propaganda aimed at enemy nations is to break down their will to fight. It seeks to lower the enemy's will to resist."[1]

In the US, the office responsible for this was called the Office of War Information. They were tasked with curating messaging through photographs, motion pictures, and storytelling that boosted the morale of those at home and abroad. Propaganda played a significant and successful role not only during WWII but in wars that followed.

Battles are not just fought on land, sea, and air like they were in WWII. We fight them every day, and our battles are first fought in the secret spaces of the soul. Once we learn to adopt the right message, we learn to align our steps with our story. This is why the gospel is so important to the life of the believer—because it's a story of predetermined victory. And if I already know I'll win, why not fight? In other words, strength and story go hand in hand. However, negative propaganda employs worry to cloud our perspective on truth—to suggest that God somehow forgot about our needs and that the battle we are currently fighting is all but lost. But God cares about what God creates. When the daily war against worry emerges, we must be armed with this truth. Since God created me, he cares about me. Good fathers provide for their children, and we have the best.

Principle 2: Worry Is a Bad Investment

Jesus's words in Matthew 6:27 should be on a bestselling graphic T-shirt. They are the echoes of countless generations who wish we'd learn from their journey. Here it is in the Vernon Translation: "Worrying is pointless." And yet, to resist worry's embrace is so much easier said than done. Worry is a tight hug in a cold season that helps us cope with the condition but never changes it.

In the world of investing, you take an amount and you sacrifice said amount based on one factor, and one factor alone—faith. Nobody invests with the expectation of loss, even if you're capable of enduring one. No, the purpose of investing is to see a return on the investment. This rule is true not only of our money but of our time, emotions, energy, and ideas. We invest; therefore, we expect something good on the other side.

Could you imagine knowing a stock will yield no return and putting your money into it anyway? How about being in a relationship for years while knowing all along it won't work out? Or my personal favorite in this season, going to the gym every day and sacrificing eating your favorite foods but knowing all along you won't hit your workout goals? It sounds bizarre to even consider why one would go to such lengths if they knew all along nothing worthy of their sacrifice awaited them on the other side.

Yet, this is what worry does best. It steals! It steals time, energy, emotions, optimism, joy, and hope, and for what? It doesn't change our condition, and it rarely changes us into a better version of ourselves. Or it's like Jesus said, rather sarcastically might I add: "Can any one of you by worrying add a single hour to your life?" (Matt. 6:27). I think we all know that was a rhetorical question. But Jesus asked it. And he is still raising it for us today. Why continue to make a bad investment with a limited return? So, commit to being a better investor of your mind and heart, and maybe, just maybe, other things will be added unto you.

Principle 3: You're Full of It—The Choice Is Yours

If you haven't picked up on it by now, Jesus was kind of forward. I know we love turn-the-other-cheek Jesus, friends-with-everybody Jesus, healer Jesus. But what about flip-over-tables Jesus? Or how about I-won't-please-everyone Jesus? And, as we saw in Matthew 6, brutally honest Jesus?

At the end of verse 30, he yet again raises a challenge for the listener of his time and ours. But this challenge is much more than insight into his dialect—it's a diagnosis. He says, "You of little faith." He recognizes that while others may dialogue with the symptoms, he speaks to the source. He named the seed of worry as a limited amount of faith.

If there's one thing I've found to be true, it's that you can't be faithful and fearful at the same time. One will take up more space than the other. What you are full of is typically determined by three daily choices—what you consume, what you commit to, and who you converse with.

Consumption happens in every area of our life, from media and entertainment to music and messaging. Remember what we learned about propaganda in modern warfare? Spiritual warfare is not very different from physical warfare in its strategy. Whatever message is loudest, clearest, and consumed the most is what we carry through life. When we lack intentionality about our consumption, we find ourselves full of narratives and notions that feed our fears and worries and not our hope and strength.

Our commitments create a daily culture too. I've always liked to say: Show me your commitments and I'll show you your values. I'll add this to that thought: If you aren't clear on your values, you'll never be committed to your vision. There is no greater enemy to vision than unclear values and poor management of commitments. Ultimately, the spaces we spend our time in aren't just passing that time; they are filling it. You leave filled with something, and if it's not faith, then it's probably fear.

Finally, our conversations are one of the most important fillers we have in life. We spend hours on phones through texts, calls, FaceTime, voice notes, and more. You'll never shake feelings if you don't get control of fillings. It's for this reason the apostle Paul writes in Romans 10:17 that "faith comes from hearing." I can't be full of faith if I'm surrounded by people who only have a vocabulary of fear. My choice to steward my conversations is critical to my ability to remain faith-full instead of fear-full.

The war against worry is a choice war before it's a change war. Many people want to worry less, change their mentality, and change their future. However, here's the truth: Change is an outcome, and choices are a solution. We learn to win the war of worry by winning the war of our choices.

So, how do we go from fear-full to faith-full? Well, the antidote is found in another New Testament passage of Scripture written by the apostle Paul. But before we get there, let's first take a step back to 1920s comics, shall we?

■ ■ ■

Are you a worrywart? Do you know someone who's a worrywart? By definition, that's someone who tends to unduly dwell on difficulty or problems beyond what's considered reasonable. Worry consumes them, consequently becoming a trait they are known for displaying—their "wart." But what if I told you that that's not how it was always defined? That its origin story, while related to this outcome, has a different context?

In 1922, cartoonist J. R. Williams drew a comic strip titled *Out Our Way*. The highly successful series ran until 1977 and featured a cast of characters that depicted American rural life. One of those characters was a young man known as Worry Wart. This particular character wasn't actually known for his own worries. Rather, he was known as the neighborhood nuisance and pest, causing worry wherever he went. Whenever Worry Wart showed up, worry showed up in the lives of others. It was only a matter of time before his presence caused stress, anxiety, frustration, and, well, worry to emerge in others.

Worry Wart resonated so much with the reality of people's everyday lives that in 1956 he was featured in his own comic book, distinct from the other characters. This edition was known as *Out Our Way with the Worry Wart*. In it, we witness not only Worry Wart's boyhood adventures but his effect on those he would encounter throughout his community. Where he went, worry followed.

Now, I'm not trying to give a lesson on comic book history and I'm certainly not suggesting that worry is not an internal issue. However, I do come with a word of caution, one that really is the underlying motivation of this entire chapter. Winning the war against worry is not just a win for you, it's a win for all those you influence. This war is a must-win because being a worrywart doesn't just influence you; it influences your home, your children, your friendships, your work environment, your marriage, your mentorship, all of it. Your worry influences your world.

That's just it. Wars are never about one generation; they are about multiple generations. Fears and worries are inherited by the next generation. If you grew up with a poverty mindset and only heard people fearing money being gone, it is likely harder to think of money as an investment tool. This is a major challenge in African American communities, as first-generation wealth builders strive to break free of "hide it under the mattress" mentalities so that we don't see money only as something to hold but something to plant in the proper places for it to increase.

However, when the only narratives we've received around money are steeped in scarcity and lack, we must apply the aforementioned principles to break free from worry in order to embrace wisdom. We must move from only knowing how to worry about money to learning how to work our money to build wealth. But these feelings and storylines are only the result of generations of disenfranchisement and discrimination. I honor the generation before us for all they were able to accomplish in spite of all they endured. And yet, their hopes and dreams for a coming generation were that we'd carry their wisdom and not their worries.

This is a war we must win. Not only for financial freedom, but for many other expressions of overcoming our worrywarts.

Our physical health is a worrywart. Our mental health is a worrywart. Our fear of commitment is a worrywart. Our culture of comparison is a worrywart. And what we carry in worry, the next generation will carry in war.

When I was eight years old, my mother frantically woke my brother and me up in the middle of the night. As she shook us from our slumber, she placed our shoes on our feet without pausing and without replacing our pajamas. With no hesitation, we ran from our rooms, through the living room, out the front door, and to our driveway, where we sat in the car, my brother and me feeling puzzled. I am certain as I replay it in my head that it must've looked like a scene from a horror movie where a family tries to escape a serial killer. By this point in my life, I had older cousins who had exposed me to Freddy Krueger, Michael Myers, and Jason Voorhees, so I reasoned that we were facing circumstances like those.

As we sat, breathing heavily in the car, my mother realized that in her haste, she forgot her car keys inside. And so she did the responsible thing. She sent me, her young son, back into the house to grab the keys. Now, I was only eight, but I was aware enough that whatever was in that house had placed the fear of God in my mother. But I was also raised in a home of radical obedience, and so, I journeyed back into the horror scene of our once-peaceful home. I ran in, quickly grabbed the keys, and dashed back out the front door. I'm sure I bolted down the last three or four steps and jumped into the car with the car keys. We left immediately and went to my aunt's house, which was not far from where we lived.

It was there that I found out what we escaped. A mouse. Yes, we fled our residence in fear and trembling because of a mouse. And that night, I was convinced mice were miniature dragons that likely breathed fire or grew in size at the smell of your fear. Whatever they did or didn't do, I was never going to find out. Because that night it was no longer just my mother's fear, it was mine too.

To this day, I am afraid of mice. That's right, I said it. And I am secure enough to handle your judgment. I have certainly matured enough to know they don't breathe fire and they don't increase in size when they smell fear. But there is still a worry in me whenever I encounter one. The worry that was transferred that night never left me. And I know a fear of mice may seem insignificant, but here's the real question: What other worries are we transferring to those we lead? What wars are they inheriting because we didn't win ours? This is a war we must win.

It is with this in mind that the apostle Paul writes a letter to the church of Philippi. He offers what I believe to be a prescription for how we can respond to worry in our life. Worry shouldn't just work on you; you should work on it. Here's what he writes in Philippians 4:6–7: "Don't worry about anything; instead, pray about everything. Tell God what you need, and thank him for all he has done. Then you will experience God's peace, which exceeds anything we can understand. His peace will guard your hearts and minds as you live in Christ Jesus" (NLT).

Is Paul saying we'll never worry? I think not. But he is encouraging us to have a plan to respond to our worry when it appears. Within these two verses lie the keys to our working on worry—four practices that we can integrate into our weekly rhythms.

Practice 1: Transparency

Paul immediately offers as a first response, "Pray about everything. Tell God what you need" (v. 6 NLT). He's suggesting that one of the ways we conquer worry is simply by sharing it.

Say what you need—and not just those things that are external or superficial. Imagine if our prayers moved from outward needs to inward support. Paul said pray about everything, which means God wants us to ask for confidence, patience, willpower, hope, resilience, all of it.

Unfortunately, our culture no longer thrives on transparency. Ours is a culture conditioned to believe that if people see the real versions of our lives, if they see our humanity, well, they will run from it. Even more concerning, I've come to learn as a pastor that most Christians don't believe God wants to meet the authentic version of them either. They are convinced that God is seeking to be impressed by their words, deeds, and lifestyle. And so we perform for God instead of presenting to God everything we need.

However, when we reveal everything, we find freedom and hope that do not easily waver when faced with worry. We don't let fear force us into the dark, because we've already brought our lives into the light. What we hide can never heal. So, we win against worry first when we choose transparency.

Practice 2: Thanksgiving

The very next thing Paul tells us to do is thank God for all he has done. This may seem simple, but this is likely the most powerful weapon against worry. Earlier we talked about propaganda and how perception is used against us in warfare. Worry wins when what we say doesn't match what we know. Read that again; I want you to digest it. Worry's best shot at winning is to get us to elevate a lie over the truth.

Practicing thanksgiving leverages your history to handle your present. It replaces the temptation of the lie with evidence of the truth. In a world filled with worry, it's important that we do not become consumed with the thoughts and temptations that chisel away at our courage. Pushing back against the narratives that create these environments is vital to our health and hope.

Here's one of the ways you can practice this: Take out a sheet of paper or go to the notes app on your phone and take ten minutes to write out a gratitude list. Without hesitation or overthinking, list out all the things you're thankful for. They could be from the previous week or from years ago. They could be small wins or big victories. But list it all out. Then fold it up and put it in the back pocket of every pair of pants you wear this week. Whenever worry shows up and presents the lie, pull out the truth and practice thanksgiving over and over again. And as you remember what God has done, you'll find faith for what God can do.

Practice 3: Trust

In conclusion, Paul encourages us by highlighting the outcomes of a life rooted in transparency and thanksgiving. He says, "Then you will experience God's peace. . . . [It] will guard your hearts and minds" (v. 7 NLT). Imagine that and exchange worry for peace. I'd bet any amount of money that there are a lot of us who'd take that trade any day of the week. And Paul says the way this is found is by trusting that the practices produce this type of promise.

Trust is not easy to come by today though. We pride ourselves on our analysis and prefer emotional walls over emotional bridges. But I am confident that worry doesn't stand a chance if we trust the plan enough to practice the prescription. Then and only then can we expect the results promised in Philippians 4.

Growing up in hospitals was no easy task, but one of the gifts in being a child while navigating tough times is that you adjust pretty quickly. Childlike faith and optimism are powerful tools, and they enable you to better control your emotions, attitude, and approach to the trial before you. I'm not saying I was never scared or never disappointed, but I was more easily convinced that a positive outcome could emerge.

Early on, I learned that I could influence my environment by my own choices, so I made a rule that no crying would happen in my room. Or I recognized that I could still make friends with other kids on my wing. I even found ways to control my entertainment by becoming a movie fanatic. But one thing I couldn't control was the medicine and the effects it had on me. Whether it was chemotherapy, antibiotics, or painkillers, all medicine is the result of a prescription. And no matter how hard it was on my body or how difficult it was to get down, I held on to a simple truth. Every prescription comes with a prognosis, a message that predicts if you do this, then you can trust this is the most anticipated outcome. And it's that message, that prescription, that gives you the will to win. Paul's prescription should be our game plan to winning the war against worry. Transparency. Thanksgiving. Trust.

No matter where you are with worry right now, you can win the war. Do not be fooled by the propaganda. God cares about what he creates, and you have weapons against worry. Yes, worry comes with your relationships, parenting, opportunities, endeavors. But just because worry joins the ride doesn't mean you have to put it in the front seat.

This is a war you can win. It's a war we must win. Lives are on the line. Not only ours, but generations that will come behind us. Our worry doesn't have to be their warfare. We choose to win today so they can live tomorrow.

SIX

What You See Is What You Get

Upon graduating high school, I attended Virginia Commonwealth University, where I majored in clinical exercise science with a concentration in pre-physical therapy. That was an extremely long way of saying I aspired to be a physical therapist or an athletic trainer.

In the early years, there was nothing problematic about my chosen degree. As with most universities, I began with general courses, which gave me the illusion that I was prepared for what was to come.

However, things took a turn in year three, as more specialized courses became mandatory, one of which was anatomy and physiology. I'll spare you the gory details, but I took that class three times. All of which ended with me receiving a W, and no, that's not a typo; it stands for "withdrawal." Not only was I not doing well but I also couldn't even finish the course. As you now know if you've read this far, I didn't end up being a physical therapist. Beyond that, I don't remember much of what I learned. But there was one lesson that I've never forgotten from that class. It's about vision.

Naturally, we give credit to our eyes for the things we see. But anatomically, our eyes don't see anything. Here's the simplified Vernon version of how sight works. (Please note, I'm not simplifying it for *you*; it was the only way I could get a few answers right on my anatomy test years ago. So, here goes nothing.)

1. Your eyes experience a message that they can't decipher independently.
2. So they send a message to the brain.
3. The brain then processes that message based on its knowledge and previous exposure.
4. It then draws a conclusion about what has been seen.

Also important to note is that the images received on the retina are upside-down, so the brain turns the images right side up. This reversal of the images is a lot like what a mirror does in a camera. Once the image is processed, the brain finalizes the interpretation of this message. In summary, your brain, not your eyes, is the greatest influence on what you see.

So, is this chapter about the biology of vision? Of course not. But this biological truth offers a powerful principle for our lives as well. Once we acknowledge that our sight is under the influence of our thoughts, we can protect, prune, and purify that which informs our vision.

Or another way to say it: When we change the way we think, we change the way we see.

This is vital for those of us becoming brave. Because a brave life is rarely a "sure life." I'm rarely sure of what I see. More often, the only thing I'm sure of is what I heard or felt God say. Consequently, if I'm not in control of my thoughts, then my filter for every opportunity, relationship, and vision is fear.

I like this idea of filters. In particular, I like to think of our thoughts as primary filters for our lives, pruning what we've deemed unnecessary and retaining the ideas that align with our preferences. For example, if my sight is only filtered through my past, that's what I'll see in situations and people. If my sight is only filtered through my pain, that's what I'll see in situations and people. If my sight is only filtered through my hopes and aspirations, that's what I'll see in situations and people. In all these filters, we find a vision of our lives that is heavily formed by our filter.

I'm sure none of us desire to repeatedly make the same mistakes. We hope to acknowledge the reality of pain or problems, as they may lead to wisdom and sensitivity. We also should be empowered by hopefulness and faith for the future. But using only one of these filters can impede a well-rounded perspective, increasing the danger of only seeing what we want to see.

It's for this reason I believe the apostle Paul wrote these words: "Do not conform to the pattern of this world, but be transformed by the renewing of your mind. Then you will be able to test and approve what God's will is—his good, pleasing and perfect will" (Rom. 12:2).

I love that Paul illuminates that there are patterns in our daily lives. Patterns of thinking, living, reacting, rationalizing, behaving. Patterns are prevalent in every part of our lives. They show up professionally, personally, relationally, even physically. I loved fried food before I had a choice; eating it was a pattern of my upbringing. I loved the sound of Sunday morning services, full of music that stirs the soul and the loud clapping on the two and four. I loved it before I chose it; it was our weekend pattern. The list goes on and on.

We have all been introduced to various patterns. Consequently, we have also been introduced to patterns of fear—routines and responses that inform our beliefs and behaviors. One of the interesting things about my childhood was the dichotomy between my two grandfathers. On my father's side was Vernon Lee Gordon Sr., who was known in our hometown as Colonel Gordon. He started as a custodian in the police department and worked his way up to the highest-ranking position of colonel, serving as the first African American officer in two local police departments.

However, his story was not without conflict and the need for courage. He would often share how he experienced abuse and intentional obstacles from others that would impede his progress. The consequence of his experience was a deep advocacy for resilience in his children and grandchildren whatever the circumstance but also a caution of White America. Certainly, this was justified per his experience, so on numerous occasions he instructed us to be careful, watch out, stay alert.

Maybe this doesn't seem like much of a shocker until you know the other side of my family. My mom's father was a White man named Milburn Turner who married my Black grandmother the first year interracial marriage was legal in the state of Virginia. My grandmother already had three Black children, the eldest of which was my mother, and my grandfather loved them as his own. They went on to have two children together, so my mother's two youngest siblings are biracial. As a family, they navigated fear of family exclusion, cultural isolation, and even physical threats on a regular basis.

My parents separated several times while I was in grade school. As such, several times I lived in the home with my

Grampa. My White Grampa. A man I deeply respected for his courage, resilience, and example. As you could imagine, this provided quite a complex in me as a child, hearing the cautions of one mighty man in my life contrasted with another mighty man in my life. Sometimes this showed up in how I embraced others. I carried an innate skepticism in some seasons that caused me to be slow to trust and try relationships with those who did not look like me. Most recently, the complex emerged as racial tensions yet again rose to the surface in 2020. I unapologetically spoke and stood for accountability, justice, and equity for Black and Brown people across America. And yet, if I'm being honest, an inner conflict constantly lived within me as I listened to narratives of mistrust emerge from race to race. I could not adopt a universal judgment and label to "others," because my own family history was rich with the example of hope and what's possible when we refuse to let the patterns be our prison.

Now, I think it's important to note that both my grandfathers ended up having a wonderful and amicable relationship. So much of who I am today is the fruit of their character and storytelling that strengthened the fabric of my identity. My story was weaved into theirs. And the truth is there were moments when I didn't know what to think even about those I love—because fears don't emerge just from what we haven't seen but also from what we have seen, heard, and been told.

Maybe your fear isn't cultural but of trusting people, taking professional risks, or trying something new. Maybe it's learning to believe in human goodness in spite of human disappointment. Paul's words are meant to be a caution, as he says that if you're not careful, you'll take on the pattern even if it's not pleasing to God or purposeful for your future. But in very short order, he tells us what we should do to resist that temptation: Be transformed by first renewing your mind.

I love the way this caution is issued in the New Living Translation of Scripture: "Don't copy the behavior and customs of this world, but let God transform you into a new person by changing the way you think. Then you will learn to know God's will for you, which is good and pleasing and perfect" (Rom. 12:2).

It's a really simple equation. A new you starts with new thinking. And new thinking is the key to new vision. Because as we've learned, you see it with your mind more than you see it with your eyes.

■ ■ ■

Such is the battle for vision. It is undoubtedly impacted by the world in front of us, behind us, and around us. You've probably heard the idiom about whether a glass is half empty or half full. Time and time again, answers vary because it all depends on how you look at the glass and, even more importantly, how you think about it.

The verse that has always been the cloud by day for me is 2 Corinthians 5:7: "For we live by faith, not by sight." Or as the New Living Translation says, "For we live by believing and not by seeing."

In short, faith must become our primary filter. We must see our lives through a prescription of our beliefs, not our problems. And as my belief grows, so too does my thinking.

So, how do we manage the way we think? Over my time of coaching and over conversations I've had with people from different generations and genders, classes and contexts, I've concluded that it often comes back to three filters. Filters we must keep pure and prepared: our eyes, our ears, and our heart, each of which affects the others.

However, awareness of these three intake valves can play a crucial role in managing moments of fear. Let's briefly take a look at each to see how we can fortify our filters.

Our Eyes

I already dedicated a considerable description to this earlier, but I'll reiterate the importance of protecting your vision. This could look like managing your content consumption, guarding yourself against comparison, and knowing when to unfollow or remove unhelpful influences. Our eyes are one of the faultiest filters in our life. And if we're not careful, we'll allow what we see to stagnate us in the pain of the present—all while lacking the ability to see the promise of the future.

Equally as important as not focusing our sight solely on the past is the acknowledgment that we haven't seen enough. With this in mind, we should be motivated to find two to three spaces of healthy vision.

Identify places that broaden your filter and set your sights on healthier and more specific goals. Find the space where you can grow, the mentor who helps you think, or the peers who hold you to the fire. Our eyes don't only compromise us when they see negativity but also when they've experienced limited activity. Put your eyes to work so that your vision can grow.

Ashley and I got engaged when we were twenty-two years old. Ashley had just received a job working as an auditor for Ernst & Young in Richmond, Virginia, and I had just accepted a position as a youth pastor in Moseley, Virginia. Yeah, I had never heard of it either. These opportunities were two hours away from our hometown, and here we were starting a new life together away from family, friends, and familiarity.

Like all young couples, we knew it all. And because we had dated since we were sixteen, marriage was going to be a breeze. (You see where this is going.) Well, it wasn't. Ashley's career was intense and required a considerable amount of travel and late nights. I barely had two pennies to scrape together in a job I loved, but I needed to spend most of my weekends accepting extra opportunities to contribute to the household.

Ashley came from a family where she had older parents and was an only child. I came from divorced parents and had siblings. Neither of us had seen a lot of marriages succeed. And if they did succeed for many years, they often didn't achieve that with a lot of happiness.

And here we were trying to create what we had never seen. We were lost trying to figure out how to merge our professional and personal lives into one.

The best gift that Baptist church in good ole Moseley, Virginia, gave wasn't a paycheck; it was a community. There were four couples in particular who surrounded us in love. Invitations to their holiday celebrations, travel opportunities, and dinners at their tables probably three times a week. They pulled us close and allowed us to see what the possibilities of love and covenant done God's way looked like.

Now, we had to do our part. We had to say yes to invitations. We had to make space in our schedule to prioritize their wisdom and presence. We had to exercise humility and ask questions and share truths about our lives. But what we got access to was a vision for what could be in our marriage. We're better because of it.

Put your eyes to work so you can see beyond your fears, frustrations, and fatigue. There's more to see.

Our Ears

It can be a simple reminder that our ears are filters that inform our lives. We've long known that music crosses cultural and experiential lines in a way that few other things can, and that's because music is universal. Have you ever watched that scene in *Rocky* where he's about to lose that middle round or the scene in *Remember the Titans* where the football team is mounting a comeback? The soundtrack tells you the story the same way the actors do; it creates a state of mind. It prompts reflection or risk-taking, danger or direction. It's moving us forward or telling us to slow down.

Here's the truth: You get to customize the soundtrack of your life. This is achieved not only through music but through being selective when exposing your ears to conversations, commentary, and content. We must choose wisely what travels through that filter. There is a passage of Scripture that always resonates with me when thinking of this: "So then faith comes by hearing, and hearing by the word of God" (Rom. 10:17 NKJV).

This passage is a simple reminder to be more selective about what we hear because faith actually comes by way of what we hear.

If you talk to athletes, they confirm that they have a gameday soundtrack—a series of songs that best prepare them for peak performance. These songs are carefully curated for energy, encouragement, and to prepare them for battle against their opponent.

A great question to consider is what the soundtrack we're playing over our lives is. Do the conversations, commentaries, and contexts we find ourselves in prepare us for a life of bravery and boldness, or fear and insecurity?

Because if faith comes by hearing, so can fear, doubt, and insecurity. Many of our lives bear the fruit of an overexposed filter. When I hear Scripture, faith, affirmation, peace, and kindness, they settle in my spirit. Eventually, those seeds come out in my language and lifestyle because they were invited to reside within. But if I allow the sounds of pessimism and fear to settle, they will eventually come out too. The filter of your ears must be a part of your becoming brave strategy. So, guard your ears, and don't apologize for being selective about the soundtrack of your life.

Our Heart

Proverbs 4:23 says, "Above all else, guard your heart, for everything you do flows from it." This passage is by far one of my favorites, as it provides a picture of what we can focus on to minimize issues that show up in our lives. We can define these issues in many ways, but they generally represent some area of our lives that's less than ideal. A place that we would hope to recalibrate or remove at the earliest opportunity.

With this in mind, I'm betting that if I were to ask if any of us would like to rid ourselves of some of our issues, there would be resounding agreement. I've never met a person who wants to carry childhood issues, professional issues, personality issues, emotional issues, and the list goes on. What Proverbs tells us in that passage is that most issues start somewhere: the heart.

Consequently, it calls us to prioritize the heart's protection at all costs. A protected heart produces a peaceful life. Now, I don't want this section to be misinterpreted as a guarantee of a life without issues. Peace is not attained by perfection but by staying in control of our perspective. Our shared experiences and human imperfections prove that pain, problems, and issues will come. However, we can live a life marked by more peace and fewer issues if we prioritize protecting our heart.

So, how do you protect your heart, you ask? That's not only a legitimate question but one that often goes unanswered. Over the years, I've formed three simple ways to cover the heart. I wouldn't consider them profound, and only you will know which to apply to the situations and seasons of your life. But I'm hoping they will provide options for your journey.

Option 1: Hide It

Your heart is valuable; act like it. Unlike other aspects of your life, the healing of the heart takes a lot of time. To prevent you from experiencing unnecessary heartache, stress, or emotional fatigue, I encourage you to take it slow with what you show. Now, before you say it, yes, I went for rhyming, and I can feel your judgment. While it may be a bit cheesy to say, just think about it. Are you showing too much of yourself too soon? This is not to say our lives should be absent of vulnerability, which requires exposure and risk. However, it is to say that specific dimensions and convictions of our hearts shouldn't be immediately accessible to all. The idea of keeping some things hidden may sound countercultural, but it is needed. We hide, not from a position of fear but from one of wisdom and caution. Let me give you two examples.

I traveled out of the country in 2018 to an area that was known for crimes against Americans. Our guide encouraged us to move our wallets from our back to our front pockets because of pickpockets. I recall thinking it highly unlikely that this would occur and thought the man was being a bit exaggerative. However, after looking at all those around me beginning to rearrange their wallets, I followed suit.

Look at any team in the NFL. The entire roster knows that the most important player on any team is their quarterback. This is a shared awareness, which is why in practice, the quarterback is given a distinctive jersey to remind players to protect this player's health at all costs.

The principle is the same in both instances. Value demands thoughtful exposure. As you navigate this next season, consider where your heart may be overexposed. Consider if there needs to be a time when you choose to limit your disclosure on social media, limit your exposure to your friends and family, and permit yourself to process some pain in private. It's okay to hide your heart for a period to protect it. It's important to note that this is not an eternal encouragement, but it can be a healthy practice in the right season.

Option 2: Heal It

The heart is a muscle; exercise it. When I was a childhood cancer patient, my health was unpredictable as new symptoms emerged throughout my treatment. Sometimes the symptoms were part of the process of the treatment at work. So, when my hair fell out, I knew why. Chemotherapy was the source. When I went to physical therapy, I was in pain, but I knew why. Every session, they were pushing through scar tissue to force flexibility. So, even when it looked bad or felt bad, I was getting better. Healing is tricky like that, as it is often disguised by the pain. And if there is no guide to tell you the purpose of your pain, you may retreat from progress.

I knew a guy named Marcus. We played basketball together on a regular basis at the gym, and he was a scoring machine. One day I was responsible for defending him, and I couldn't help but notice that several of his fingers looked disjointed. With genuine concern, I inquired if he had experienced an injury recently and if he should be playing. He began informing me that the injuries were actually older issues from his adolescence. When it was time to get his fingers treated, the pain of the doctor's visit and the prospect of missing a year of playing for his high school team prompted him to avoid treatment. Then, before he knew it, years had gone by and he learned to cope with the condition, although it was never properly treated and repaired.

Many don't heal because they avoid the discomfort of the present. Healing can be heavy, hard, and can even hurt, but it's healthier to heal than to hold on. Sometimes your heart needs to heal before it can return to regular activity. So, exercise it with caution and with care.

Option 3: Handle It

The heart is fragile; make it known. If you've ever fractured a bone or endured a sprain before, you place the affected area in a sling or cast to protect it. Every time someone comes close, they gingerly approach you to avoid causing you further injury.

When we move, it is common to label the boxes containing items that need extra care in transit. Everyone knows to pick up and put down those boxes carefully so as not to break the contents within. Why? Because fragility requires visibility.

Letting those closest to you know you're in a fragile place is not weakness; it's wisdom. It's allowing them the opportunity to increase their sensitivity in transition and their awareness in approach. It's how they will know to partner with you in protection so that your heart can be healthy. They can't help with what they don't know. So often we are tempted to try to handle our hearts all on our own. But life is not designed for every weight to be lifted independently. Our ability to allow helping hands and pure hearts to assist us in certain seasons is sometimes the strongest action we can take.

Ultimately, what you see is what you get. But we don't just see the world through our eyes. We see the world around us through our filters, each filter playing a significant role in how we plan for peace and progress in our lives. And we see the world through our faith, for we walk by faith and not by sight.

Keep walking. Keep believing.

SEVEN

Somewhere Over the Rainbow

There are movies, and then there are classics. If we ever get a chance to grab a cup of coffee together, I'd love to debate with you some of the best movies of all time.

But for this chapter's namesake, let me tell you what I believe is one of the greatest movies of all time: *The Wizard of Oz*. It's a story of the unknown, adventure, and hope—a tale of self-discovery and a community that triumphs over evil. There's no debating it's top ten.

If you've been under a rock and don't know the storyline here, let me give you the CliffsNotes. Dorothy, a young girl from Kansas, is magically transported to the land of Oz. She is initially greeted by the people of Munchkinland, my favorite of whom were the Lollipop Guild. Oh, the memories.

Somewhere Over the Rainbow

She finds out that the way home is a road, specifically a yellow brick road, that she's to follow to the Emerald City, where the great and powerful wizard will tell her how to get back to Kansas.

All of this is set in motion, however, by an argument at the beginning of the movie that leaves Dorothy unsettled. While wrestling with life's uncertainties, she begins to sing a song called "Over the Rainbow." Odds are you know the song, as it is one of the most well-known songs in the world to this day. But beyond its commercialization, the song's origins have an even deeper meaning.

Naturally, many of us are familiar with Judy Garland's rendition in the movie or the version sung by Israel "IZ" Kamakawiwoʻole. But we might not know about the origins of the song. It was written in 1939 by a Russian-Jewish immigrant named Isidore Hochberg. The music was composed by Harold Arlen, a Lithuanian immigrant living in New York at the time. The song's inspiration came from the many decades of pogroms and persecution that European Jews lived under. When *The Wizard of Oz* released in 1939, Jews were coming under increased hostility as their freedoms were being taken away, their identities were being questioned, and many were being put in false imprisonment throughout Nazi Germany. Unable to escape their reality, the song became an ode to hope and inner freedom amid what would later be called the Holocaust over the next six years across Europe.

Considering these origins, lyrics like "away above the chimney tops" take on new meaning as we look back on the horrors of the concentration camps and the many needless casualties suffered. In the midst of darkness and despair, a song that points to a future of possibility and dreams provides powerful imagery to a people caught in impossible circumstances.

As I've grown older, I've found that these lyrics continue to ring true in the stories of countless human experiences. Moments where a distant hope and an unclear journey meet quiet confidence and a proclaimed future. An assurance that somewhere out there, something better awaits. This school of thought has become the ultimate navigation tool in times of disappointment and confusion. I've come to learn that most challenges don't require our insight as much as they require our endurance. That life doesn't always need our opinions as much as it does our optimism. Without these tools, our emotions would constantly point out the cloudy skies and not the emerging rainbows. And we'd lose the ability to see and shape our future beyond our fears.

Now, this may sound like idealistic work, but it's really what we all do each and every day of our lives. We mold our world with our words. We shape our experience with our expectations. Every time we say "I can't" or "That's impossible" or "That's just the way it is," we are setting an expectation for our existence.

Certainly don't assume this is just the by-product of our words. This reality is also found proof positive in our habits. We mold and shape our lives when we choose binge-watching over binge-reading, sugar and salt over smoothies and vegetables, and sleeping in over working out. All of these daily choices show up in our futures, and psychology has consistently proven they affect our emotions. Our overall mental and physical health, consumption of media and knowledge, and perceived control over daily decision-making play a part in how we feel about ourselves and the lives being shaped before us. If this is in fact true, that means our daily choices determine our future experience. And our daily commentary impacts our conception.

The Scriptures have certainly echoed this truth time after time. Proverbs 18:21 says, "The tongue has the power of life and death, and those who love it will eat its fruit," and Psalm 141:3 says, "Set a guard over my mouth, Lord; keep watch over the door of my lips."

In James, Jesus's half brother paints a powerful picture of the tongue and its influence in our life through a series of metaphors. I think it's important to see these at length.

> When we put bits into the mouths of horses to make them obey us, we can turn the whole animal. Or take ships as an example. Although they are so large and are driven by strong winds, they are steered by a very small rudder wherever the pilot wants to go. Likewise, the tongue is a small part of the body, but it makes great boasts. Consider what a great forest is set on fire by a small spark. The tongue also is a fire, a world of evil among the parts of the body. It corrupts the whole body, sets the whole course of one's life on fire, and is itself set on fire by hell.
>
> All kinds of animals, birds, reptiles and sea creatures are being tamed and have been tamed by mankind, but no human being can tame the tongue. It is a restless evil, full of deadly poison.
>
> With the tongue we praise our Lord and Father, and with it we curse human beings, who have been made in God's likeness. Out of the same mouth come praise and cursing. My brothers and sisters, this should not be. Can both fresh water and salt water flow from the same spring? My brothers and sisters, can a fig tree bear olives, or a grapevine bear figs? Neither can a salt spring produce fresh water. (3:3–12)

If there's a central takeaway here, it's that words matter. Getting control of our words is getting control of our life. And if there's one thing fear compromises most, it's our words. Whenever we face fear, we're not just in a war of will, we're in a war of words.

People often ask me how they can read the Bible every day and how it adds value to their life. I tell them that I am constantly drawn to the relevance of Scripture to our everyday lives. Don't get me wrong, I love leadership books, case studies, autobiographies, all of it. But if you're asking me, the Bible is second to none in teaching us how to win at every area of life. Sometimes we learn from the obedience, successes, and positive outcomes of those we read about. Other times, we learn from their mistakes, mishaps, and missed opportunities.

No group models this truth better than the children of Israel. If you'd allow me, I'll share a bit of backstory to offer context. The Israelites were held in Egyptian captivity for four hundred years. These years were filled with prayers and petitions for freedom. One day, God sent a deliverer, a man named Moses, to free them from their captors and to lead them to a promised land.

Through a series of miracles and moments, the most memorable being the parting of the Red Sea, they moved beyond waiting and into the wilderness. And as they moved through the wilderness, they were headed to Canaan. This journey was slated to take approximately eleven days but ended up as forty years of wandering. What caused this forty-year delay? There was one singular moment that became the catalyst, and it's found in the following verses:

> They came back to Moses and Aaron and the whole Israelite community at Kadesh in the Desert of Paran. There they reported to them and to the whole assembly and showed them the fruit of the land. They gave Moses this account: "We went into the land to which you sent us, and it does flow with milk and honey! Here is its fruit. But the people who live there are powerful, and the cities are fortified and very large. We even saw descendants of Anak there. The Amalekites live in the Negev; the Hittites, Jebusites and Amorites live

in the hill country; and the Canaanites live near the sea and along the Jordan."

Then Caleb silenced the people before Moses and said, "We should go up and take possession of the land, for we can certainly do it."

But the men who had gone up with him said, "We can't attack those people; they are stronger than we are." And they spread among the Israelites a bad report about the land they had explored. They said, "The land we explored devours those living in it. All the people we saw there are of great size. We saw the Nephilim there (the descendants of Anak come from the Nephilim). We seemed like grasshoppers in our own eyes, and we looked the same to them." (Num. 13:26–33)

These verses are crucial to living a life beyond fear. In many ways, they serve as a traffic sign as we travel our own roads to promise. Their primary offering is awareness that we must maintain in ourselves the fortitude to frame commentary and commitments that are not overrun by our emotions. I once heard someone say, "Emotions make for a great passenger but a horrible driver." The seat we give our emotions speaks a great deal to the influence they have and to whether we stay on the path toward promise or find permanence in our pain. Here are three cautions we can extract from the delayed promise of the Israelites.

Caution 1: Trust the Fruit, Not the Fear

It's one thing to be afraid when you don't have evidence of what you're looking for. It's an entirely different thing to have evidence and let it be discredited by insecurity. That's what happens to the children of Israel. They see the fruit and it is good. The fruit represents the confirmation of God's promise that they will enter a land flowing with milk and honey.

Yet, most of the people become convinced that the promise isn't worth the process. They allow the first sight of opposition—occupants in the space they are headed to—to minimize their forward movement. They follow their fear and not the fruit.

For clarity, *trust* is the operative word here. In every crossroads of your life, you will be forced to decide which to follow: faith or fear. Want to really be challenged? What's safe will often sound sure. But surety is not the goal of a follower of Jesus. Steadfast is the heart's posture we should pursue and protect.

There are giants. And there is fruit. There is opposition. And there is opportunity.

Sometimes all you'll have is a piece of the promise. Learning to focus our attention on what God has promised and not on the fear of what we're facing is vital to our progress. Trusting God and ourselves is essential to the brave new world we're being called to.

Caution 2: Bigger Isn't Always Better

Getting everybody on board is not always best. Sometimes, just getting the right people on board is all you need. Very often, in our attempt to be inclusive and diplomatic, we invite too many voices to the table.

I'm all for wisdom in a multitude of counsel. Just make sure that counsel is actually wise. Moses selected twelve spies to go into the land and inspect its fruit. That was their assignment. However, when they returned, ten of the twelve included additional findings in their report. The findings related to the people there—their size, their risk, and even their assumed intent. Of course, this was without conversation with the aforementioned giants.

Okay, can I take a quick hermeneutic detour for just a moment? I'd love to share with you something I think is so interesting biblically.

When Moses is leading the people of Israel into the promised land, he sends twelve spies, representative of each tribe, into the land. Ten of the twelve become problematic and divisive within the camp. As we now know, this sets in motion a forty-year wandering in the wilderness. Two of the twelve, however, were full of confidence and trust in God's promise.

At the conclusion of Moses's tenure as leader, his successor, Joshua, is given the same assignment to lead the people into the promised land. Do you know how many spies he sent to inspect the land? Two!

He learned the lesson that bigger isn't always better. More people, more opinions, and more affirmations do not always equal efficiency and effectiveness. Sometimes you'll need twelve, and other times you only need two.

Caution 3: Watch Your Mouth—What You Say Is What You'll See

My mother used to say, "If you ain't got nothing good to say, don't say nothing at all." I used to hate it when she said that, but boy, did she have some wisdom. As we've learned, our words have power, and whatever you're saying is what you're going to start seeing.

In all fairness, we often use talking as a way to process our own fears without realizing we're sowing seeds of fear in others. The consequence? We create echo chambers of confirmation bias. "I think this way" quickly becomes "We think this way." And when "we" think in a certain way, then "we" must be right.

The Bible says the spies spread a bad report among the land. After all they had seen God do to get them there, after finding the evidence confirming everything God said about their promise, ten leaders compromised the culture with their conversations. Because it's our mouth that gets us in the most trouble.

Anytime you are facing fear, be careful about what you say regarding three things:

1. *Your report.* Stop diminishing what you find. If God is showing you fruit, favor, success, increase, opportunity, or open doors, you don't have to dilute it with fear talk. Watch your report, or you'll start to see more of the struggle than the success.
2. *Your challenge.* Stop giving so much attention and conversation to your challenge, allowing your imagination to create outcomes that are not verified by experience. What may happen should never be more powerful than what has happened.
3. *Yourself.* How you talk about yourself matters. In particular, we should never allow our idea of ourselves to supersede God's idea of us. The spies said, "We seemed like grasshoppers in our own eyes" (Num.13:33). It was not what others said about them that squandered their potential but what they said about themselves. And if you say it enough, that's what you'll start to see.

How does this happen? How do we find the promise and still make a plan to avoid it? When we let fear speak freely, that's what happens every time. So we must grab hold of our words if we want to win the season.

■ ■ ■

For the last few years, I've served as a convener for an organization called Uptick, which is committed to creating Jesus-shaped leaders for the next generation. Each year at the end of our cohort's journey, participants are encouraged to write a future story, which is a kind of testament to who they are becoming as a result of the year's journey. It's always amazing to hear the stories of individuals whose starting points don't become their resting places, of leaders who bring insecurities, questions, and inner conflict to the table and leave with some of them still present but also with another piece to the puzzle, a picture of possibilities.

We all get the opportunity to write a future story of our lives. Don't give emotions and experiences the power to take that privilege away from you. It's your inheritance as a human being and a creation of God.

Throughout history, great leaders have leveraged the power of words to shape the world. Voices of liberation have shaped civil rights, platforming unseen pain and inequality. Voices of resolve and inspiration have empowered people to stand sure-footed in the midst of fear and uncertainty. Voices of faith have pointed the way to a life of deeper purpose and principle, spurring many to a life of Christian discipleship.

Reflecting on this led me back to timeless speeches and sermons such as:

Sojourner Truth's "Ain't I a Woman?" from 1851
Abraham Lincoln's "Gettysburg Address" from 1863
Nelson Mandela's "I Am Prepared to Die" from 1964
Martin Luther King Jr.'s "The Drum Major Instinct" from 1968
Maya Angelou's "Still I Rise" from 1978
Francis Chan's "The Power of a Quiet Life" from 2024

These moments, and many others throughout history, have shaped culture and conversations through generations, piercing calloused hearts and exposing the cultural and spiritual sinkholes we've built many of our ideals on.

In 1910, just after his presidency, Theodore Roosevelt traveled to Paris to give a speech titled "Citizenship in a Republic." If that's unfamiliar to you, it's because it's affectionately come to be known by a different title, one that captures the segment that has resonated with generation after generation: "The Man in the Arena." Within it, he shares these words:

> It is not the critic who counts; not the man who points out how the strong man stumbles, or where the doer of deeds could have done them better. The credit belongs to the man who is actually in the arena, whose face is marred by dust and sweat and blood; who strives valiantly; who errs, who comes short again and again, because there is no effort without error and shortcoming; but who does actually strive to do the deeds; who knows great enthusiasms, the great devotions; who spends himself in a worthy cause; who at the best knows in the end the triumph of high achievement, and who at the worst, if he fails, at least fails while daring greatly, so that his place shall never be with those cold and timid souls who neither know victory nor defeat.[1]

In full transparency, these words have been a North Star for me on many occasions. Moments when external opinions and criticisms have produced second-guessing. When the weight of winning and warfare has felt like too heavy a burden to carry. But in these words, we find both the permission to pursue purpose imperfectly and the permission to fail in pursuit. Simply put, to dare greatly.

Daring greatly means we fail publicly at times. It may mean we are left exposed, vulnerable, and without protection from the opinions of critics.

But failure is not final. Despite what many may think, failure is an invitation to improvement. And improvement an invitation to insight. And insight an invitation to imagination about what could be in our lives.

How do we shape our world with our words? There are five key disciplines to incorporate in your journey. And I don't want to rush past the word *discipline*. Taming the tongue is a discipline. In a world where we can say whatever we want, the wisest among us know the difference between wanting to be heard and wanting to be helpful.

Discipline 1: Say What You Mean and Mean What You Say

This is a common but important phrase to embody in our day-to-day life. The true advocacy of these words is for intentionality. Am I simply speaking to be heard or am I speaking for change? At what level of intention am I using my words?

When we speak with intention, it begins to shape our lives in ways that allow for greater integrity and impact. Our words become mile markers on the journey to becoming brave.

Discipline 2: Speak Scripture

This is easily one of the most important and lost practices of modern culture.

What is Jesus facing in the wilderness when the devil shows up? Temptation, sure, but two of the three temptations are rooted in fear and identity. "Are you really who you say you are? You're going to miss out if you don't take this offer to have all these kingdoms." And so on and so on. And each time, Jesus doesn't respond with his feelings or clap back with attitude. He responds with Scripture.

Learning how to speak Scripture into your life, over your life, and in response to your life is a vital discipline. I'd encourage everyone to find four or five Scriptures for every season and memorize them. Make them the thing you say over and over again when you feel overwhelmed, afraid, insecure, defeated, confused. Speak Scripture.

Discipline 3: Speak to Your Mountains and Not About Them

We all need a place where we can get it all out. To vent, dump, and express ourselves. I think that's an important practice. However, it is not the only healthy thing we can do. As a matter of fact, I think that while that may be used in case of emergency, it should be our secondary response.

What should be our first? To speak to the mountain.

There's this amazing moment when Jesus is walking with the disciples and they begin a conversation about faith. He says, "If anyone says to this mountain, 'Go, throw yourself into the sea,' and does not doubt in their heart but believes that what they say will happen, it will be done for them" (Mark 11:23). Jesus was trying to get them to understand that there is no power in what you talk about. There is only power in what you speak to.

We live in a culture that is comfortable talking about fears, frustrations, people, and the list goes on. But when was the last time you spoke "to" the mountain of your life, calling it out by name, saying this must go, this must bow, this must shift, this must change, it must? Speak to the mountain, not just about it.

Discipline 4: Slow Down

Public Service Announcement: The one who speaks first is not the one who speaks well. As a pastor, I am asked weekly what

I think about a trending topic. Very often, I've had no time to develop my own thoughts on the matter. The temptation is to feel that to slow down is to not show up.

However, Jesus very often slowed down. Before he shows up, speaks up, or stands up, he's found to be in a quiet place with the Father, allowing presence to precede proclamation. Over and over again.

Our culture is always saying too much, too soon, too fast. And we continuously consume thoughts and commentary that weren't thought out or had incomplete theses at best. Exercise the discipline to slow down.

Discipline 5: Let Silence Speak for You

Here's a bit of cultural contradiction for you: You don't have to speak at all. Silence is not simply reserved for monasteries but should be a weekly rhythm. I try to aim for an hour of silence a week. That's not to say there aren't other moments when I'm quiet or working. I'm not speaking of that.

I mean intentional time of solitude and silence without the cloudiness of work or demands.

Silence is the language of the soul. To enter silence is to initiate a conversation with the matters of the heart in a way that sharing out loud cannot accomplish.

Incorporation of this discipline will allow you to speak, when led, with greater clarity, consistency, and communion with the Father. Sometimes your lack of response will be a greater testament than you could imagine.

Ultimately, let's hold to the final words of that timeless song: "If happy little bluebirds fly beyond the rainbow, why, oh why can't I?"[2] Although it has been said, it must be remembered that one of the most powerful weapons against fear is our own words to our future.

Why not you? Why not now?

Our song is not only the story as is but the story we hope to see. Let's find our way back to the yellow brick road. There's a future waiting that we'll be proud we fueled with the right words.

EIGHT

Power to the People

Recently, I've been thinking about going back to school to get my doctorate. Candidly, I wasn't an avid learner in grade school, but as I've grown older, I recognize I miss the academy. The stretching of my mind and methods and the challenging of my default ideals.

I fell in love with learning in seminary. I got my master of divinity from the Samuel DeWitt Proctor School of Theology of Virginia Union University. I valued those late nights and long days of dialogues and deadlines. It was an arena of public thought where gladiators exchanged ideas and positions for sport and not for a speech or sermon, where confirmation bias and echo chambers were hard to come by. Those days seem far behind me at times, but I miss them.

Now, what I'm about to say next will be celebrated by some and disagreeable to others. But I'm confident I'm not alone in this. Okay, here goes nothing.

I loved group projects.

Now, if you're triggered by these words, it's likely because you've had some traumatic group project experiences. One of those memories of you doing all the work and then everyone else showing up and getting the credit. I'd like to apologize to you on behalf of all of us who participate, contribute, and collaborate.

In my experience, however, these have been some of the most meaningful expressions of ideas. Different gifts, styles of learning, and interpretations partnering to present a shared idea is so much fun. And I think it's so like God.

What do you mean, Vernon? Well, God seemed to be keen on giving out group projects throughout Scripture—experiences that were evaluated on the basis of the group, not just the basis of the individual.

In the last chapter, we highlighted Moses and his assignment to lead the children of Israel through the wilderness and into the promised land. But God doesn't take Moses to Canaan alone; he sends him with other people. And it's the people in the camp who are full of doubt, insecurity, and reservations that set in motion a forty-year delay.

But there are also positive examples of people playing a part in purpose and partnership. Ruth tells Naomi, "Do not urge me to leave you or to return from following you. For where you go I will go, and where you lodge I will lodge. Your people shall be my people, and your God my God" (Ruth 1:16 ESV).

I love this idea of Ruth telling Naomi, "I'm with you. Wherever you are and whoever you're rocking with, I'm there too. Whatever this next season holds, we're facing it together."

Or there's Paul in the New Testament consistently highlighting people who play an essential role in the spread of the gospel message. We know that at the time of Christianity's spread, the "stars of the league," as I like to call them, were Paul, Timothy, and Barnabas. And yet Paul acknowledges a lot of people who came alongside the mission to manage, minister, and meet the needs of others.

> In Romans 16:6, he says, "Greet Mary, who worked very hard for you."
> In Romans 16:12, he says, "Greet Tryphena and Tryphosa, those women who work hard in the Lord."
> In Philippians 4:2–3, he says, "I plead with Euodia and I plead with Syntyche. . . . They have contended at my side in the cause of the gospel."
> In 2 Timothy 4:11, he says, "Get Mark . . . because he is helpful to me in my ministry."
> In Colossians 4:12, he praises Epaphras, who is "always wrestling in prayer for you."
> In Romans 16:3, he says, "Greet Priscilla and Aquila, my co-workers in Christ Jesus."
> In Romans 16:1–2, he says, "I commend to you our sister Phoebe, a deacon of the church in Cenchreae. I ask you to receive her in the Lord in a way worthy of his people and to give her any help she may need from you, for she has been the benefactor of many people, including me."

These are all people who Paul commends for their collaboration, impact, and influence. Consequently, we see that Paul's calling was not enough to fulfill his assignment. Paul needed people.

In the spirit of beating a dead horse, I'd like to further emphasize this point. Admittedly, you may already be sold on this idea, but it would feel like spiritual malpractice not to reference Jesus's ministry and his partnership with people. When Jesus sets out to prepare the world to carry out heaven's agenda on earth, he called twelve men to follow him, learn from him, and live and lead with him. Often when we look at the Twelve, I think we see them as idly joining the journey with little to do but take notes and walk from town to town. However, the Bible offers a slightly different picture when we peer in a bit closer. We see several of them busy with work supporting the ministry with diverse gifts and responsibilities.

Judas was taking care of the money: "Now he said this, not because he cared about the poor [for he had never cared about them], but because he was a thief; and since he had the money box [serving as treasurer for the twelve disciples], he used to pilfer what was put into it" (John 12:6 AMP).

Jesus sent Peter to fish for a coin. He later sent disciples ahead of the group to find somewhere for them to have the last supper. And we see women who were underwriters of Jesus and the disciples' journey: "Soon afterward Jesus began a tour of the nearby towns and villages, preaching and announcing the Good News about the Kingdom of God. He took his twelve disciples with him, along with some women who had been cured of evil spirits and diseases. Among them were Mary Magdalene, from whom he had cast out seven demons; Joanna, the wife of Chuza, Herod's business manager; Susanna; and many others who were contributing from their own resources to support Jesus and his disciples" (Luke 8:1–3 NLT).

Even Jesus had help! Because people have always been a part of God's design for purpose.

Becoming brave is a personal project. Staying brave is a group project. There's power in finding your people.

The movie *300* recalls the story of the three hundred Spartans who gloriously mounted a defense against the king of Persia, Xerxes. The Persian army was considered the largest army in the world at that time. How did the Spartans mount this impressive defense time and time again, defying the odds with only a small band of dedicated soldiers, baffling the larger army?

In a scene that precedes the first battle, a Spartan with a physical disability requests to be a part of the battle. King Leonidas denies his request on the merit of their battle strategy. He communicates that the Spartans fight as a "single impenetrable unit" called a phalanx. A single weak spot, and the defense shatters. However, when all are in position and protecting one another, that is the source of their strength.

The truth is that most bravery isn't built on individual merit alone. The people we bring into our life either add or take away power. This means the good selection of companionship and connection is vital to our lived experience. In most of our origin stories, there was an encourager along the way, sometimes an intercessor or an instigator of purpose and potential. A voice that wouldn't allow us to bow to fear but to face it and fight it. Connection with others is a catalyst to becoming the best version of ourselves. It is in connection that we find the chiseling of character and commitments that ultimately shapes us into stronger versions of ourselves.

Social psychologist and expert on connection and vulnerability Brené Brown highlights in her famous TED Talk, "The Power of Vulnerability," that "connection is why we're here. We are hardwired to connect with others, it's what gives purpose and meaning to our lives, and without it there is suffering."[1]

There is no shortage right now of research confirming this truth that a life absent of connection is a life lacking fullness. Even more, there have been several studies confirming that social isolation registers in the same region of the brain as physical pain does. It hurts to not have your people.

Bravery is not an unlimited resource. It is not something we're born with, nor is it something that is bottled up and sold as a commodity. It is a seasonal supply that is refilled through experiences, expectations, and empowerment. It is the by-product of bold prayers, deep belief, and unselfish people who freely share of their testimony and trust in God.

I grew up in a tight-knit community in Chesapeake, Virginia. My religious experience was anchored in one of those small family churches. The first church building I remember us having was positioned squarely on the heels of train tracks. During services, it would be so loud that the preacher would have to pause while the train passed by. That building had no central AC or heat. In the summer, we were at risk of heatstroke. In the winter, my cousins and I would sit tightly together in the row, attached to each other's hips to ensure full coverage of the blanket that warmed us all. However, hot summers, cold winters, and loud locomotives were no match for the faith of our forefathers and foremothers.

One of the segments of our services would be the testimony service. During this time, all people would be invited to share personal reflections on God's goodness in their life. As I think back on those days, I am in awe of the unwavering confidence they had in what God did or what they were believing him to do. They would often seem unfazed by financial challenges, medical reports, or unexpected seasons.

I didn't appreciate it much then, as there were many days I was hoping they would move on quickly so we could progress toward the end of the service. As the years have passed,

I find myself reflecting on their faith. In many ways, I'm convinced that my bravery was first built in the sauna of their stories, fashioned in the freezing tundra of their testimonies we witnessed week in and week out. They taught us how to believe. They taught us how to behave. They taught us how to become brave!

But they also showed us that bravery is a team sport. As they would respond, celebrate, pray, and follow up, they modeled that your victory is our victory. Their communal empowerment signaled to the world and to each other a tethered resilience not built on the back of one but on the bridge to many. Seeing their faith always reminds me of the truth Solomon shares in Ecclesiastes 4:

> Two are better than one,
>   because they have a good return for their labor:
> If either of them falls down,
>   one can help the other up.
> But pity anyone who falls
>   and has no one to help them up.
> Also, if two lie down together, they will keep warm.
>   But how can one keep warm alone?
> Though one may be overpowered,
>   two can defend themselves.
> A cord of three strands is not quickly broken. (vv. 9–12)

Life with the right people equals power. And power is what will help you up when you fall. Help you stay warm when you're cold. Help you defend yourself when overpowered. Help you become brave and stay brave as you journey to your future.

When I was growing up, my grandmother ran one of the most prestigious home day cares in our community. By prestigious, I mean that if you were born between 1980 and 2000, you probably did a stint. My grandmother is a no-nonsense woman who valued discipline, devotion to God, and learning. She might not have had the fancy building or the biggest budget, but when you went to Turner Family Daycare, you were going to be challenged to think.

Certainly, this showed up in math, science, and reading. But one of the things I hated when growing up is that every summer she'd make us memorize all the presidents. Every one of them, in order. Please don't ask me to recite them now because that would be a short exercise.

As you know, every four years in America we elect a president. Now, I know what you're thinking. *Vernon, tell us something we don't know.* Give me a few sentences and I'll attempt to. I recognize that the exercise of knowing presidents not only was the practice of my childhood but it's the posture of my adulthood. I'm involved in the civic responsibility of voting. I know who my president is each term. But recently I was challenged by a different exploration.

Every four years we don't just elect a president—we also confirm a new cabinet. Okay, here's the question: Do you know what the president's cabinet is?

The cabinet is an advisory body made up of leaders of fifteen executive departments. These persons are chosen by the president, generally because of their experience and alignment with the president's agenda, and confirmed by the Senate for checks and balances and proper vetting.

In George Washington's cabinet there were only four original members: Secretary of State Thomas Jefferson, Secretary of Treasury Alexander Hamilton, Secretary of War Henry Knox, and Attorney General Edmund Randolph.

But whether there were four or fifteen cabinet members, our country has always been governed by a simple truth: No one person knows it all. We all have limitations and blind spots, and only with the help of other people can a president brave the responsibility of guiding us forward as a nation.

If there was anyone in the Bible who knew what it meant to be brave, it was David. We talked about David's journey in chapter 1 and how his first giants showed up in family and in leadership. However, there's more to consider about David's story and example. I mean, how many of us actually know what happened after Goliath? I think in many ways the beauty and power of David's story is how, in season after season, he doesn't just rely on ability, he also relies on people for wisdom, support, guidance, friendship, and more.

The arc of his journey and the nuance of it is why he is easily one of my favorite biblical representatives of a life beyond fear. For while we highlight his strength in battle, it is his humanity that bridges with our existence. And it's that humanity we must address before this section is over.

Courage does not purge us of our humanity, but it can conceal it. That concealer may help us endure battles, but it cannot help us endure life. We must learn to manage the tension of carrying strength and needing support, being full of courage and needing care, producing power and experiencing pain.

Throughout David's life, he models for us how to find power in the right people. As we journey through his life, let's look at the five types of people we all need to have in our lives to succeed.

Catalysts

The first time we meet David in 1 Samuel 16, he's not a highly regarded individual. There was a prophet named Samuel who was serving the king of the time, Saul. God speaks to him, letting him know that Saul no longer has his blessing and that the next king will be one of Jesse's sons. So he journeys to Jesse's house and asks him to arrange all his sons in front of him so that he may discern, decide, and anoint the next king. One after another, Jesse sends his sons forward. Seven in total are presented and rejected by Samuel.

Samuel sits confused and asks, "Are these all the sons you have?" Jesse admits to having an eighth son, David, and sends for him. David has been out in the field taking care of the sheep. When he arrives, do you know what happens? Samuel looks at him and declares that he is the one to be anointed.

Now, this is significant because Samuel sets in motion a calling on David's life that is not immediately experienced but merely expressed. Think about it. When Samuel leaves, he doesn't go to make David king; that's beyond his control. He simply planted the seed and prophesied to what would be. David has to go back to the field and ponder the idea of himself and his potential. He must wrestle with his own abilities, cultural limitations, family dynamics, age, and appearance, and somehow in that melting pot, he has to find the fire that's just been started in him.

Don't miss this reality: David didn't start the fire. David didn't start the vision. David didn't start the desire. Samuel did. Samuel was the catalyst God chose for who David would become.

There will be times in all our lives when people will become the catalyst to possibilities, sometimes through the words they share or the exposure they offer.

What do we need a catalyst to do?

- See our potential and possibilities
- Encourage us to believe bigger for ourselves

- Say things that may seem unattainable to us in the present
- Show up in our lives to speak to our future
- Serve as voices but not always as guides

Contenders

What propels David to popularity and consideration for national leadership? One simple word: *Goliath*. No Goliath, no chance.

The presence of opposition is what provides the opportunity for progress.

Goliath is necessary, not just in David's life but in ours. Some giants are really invitations to highlight skills, wisdom, and abilities you've cultivated in the dark, and the setting enables you to bring them to the light.

The Goliath your company is facing could be an invitation for you to step into the square as the problem solver your CEO has been looking for.

The Goliath your family is facing could be an invitation for you to pave a new path for generations to come.

The Goliath your faith is facing could be an invitation for you to deepen your trust in God and see just how much he trusts you.

Champions are enshrined in the heat of battle. Did they win when it counted? And did they win in a fashion that confirms their dominance?

I mean, many are still asking if the Lakers' 2020 bubble championship counts. Do we think Jordan had an easier path to the finals? The 2015 injury-ridden Cavs lost to the Golden State Warriors, but even I could have played on that team. Does it matter? I'm not trying to create a conflict; I'm simply highlighting the fact that we judge the champion by the contender.

And maybe the challenge, conflict, or contender of your life is a gift to usher you into your future.

What do we need contenders to do?

- Give us opportunities to stretch our faith
- Push us to maximize our potential
- Apply pressure for the sake of purpose
- Present fear on one side but faith on the other

Confidants

None of us need to be contending all the time. It's one thing to be popular; it's another thing to feel known. And sometimes you just want to go where people know your name—kind of like what the theme song from the classic sitcom *Cheers* says. Now, this is not just a reference to following or popularity. In *Cheers*, this was a place where people came to be vulnerable, supported, and cheered on.

In David's life and in ours, we all need confidants. People who know us deeply and personally. Places that don't require us to be king or queen, leader or visionary, strong or wise—just human.

Following the defeat of Goliath, David began serving in the army of Saul. Saul's son Jonathan and David became close friends. Scripture defines the depth of their friendship:

> As soon as he had finished speaking to Saul, the soul of Jonathan was knit to the soul of David, and Jonathan loved him as his own soul. And Saul took him that day and would not let him return to his father's house. Then Jonathan made a covenant with David, because he loved him as his own soul. (1 Sam. 18:1–3 ESV)

There was a depth found in David's relationship with Jonathan that he needed as his life rapidly changed. He went from the fields to the palace, from being forgotten to being famous. That's jolting, and Jonathan, who was raised in it, connected as a brother to support David.

Confidants allow you to remove the armor and become an ally to your soul. They don't care about how many battles you've won; they want to know where the scars are left on your soul. Confidants become a place of refuge and refueling. Without them, we run on empty and eventually run out. We run out of strength, answers, ideas, resolve.

David's connection to Jonathan is a reminder to us all that we need covenant relationships not just for marriage but for life.

What do we need confidants to do?

- Provide a safe space for our humanity
- Serve as listeners and advisers
- Show up when we need them
- Feel for us as a person, not the product we produce
- Be trustworthy with all aspects of our life

Champions

Here's one of my firmly held beliefs: I believe everybody has one friend. An individual who is ready to fight for you as soon as you call. They don't need to know if it was your fault, what the backstory is, or any additional information. They just need to know when and where to show up. For some of us, we heard those words literally and physically, and some of us interpreted them metaphorically. I'm not here to judge either. It's just a simple reminder that there's nothing like the feeling of people who are loyal to us.

Champions are ready to fight for your dream, idea, reputation, or opportunity at a moment's notice. And David was not without his own champions. They were actually called David's mighty men (2 Sam. 23:8).

David's mighty men were an elite force who helped him conquer territory and build the kingdom once he eventually became king. Their bravery is noted throughout Scripture, and without them David would not have become the king he was. At some point, David had to move from relying on his own slingshot to relying on the support of others.

Be careful when you're trying to sustain a show of strength by yourself. Every great leader and every healthy life allow people to come alongside and fight with them. You've heard it said before that there is strength in numbers. You don't need all people, but the right people at the right time can help you every time.

What do we need champions to do?

- Bring specific skills and experience to the season
- Take work, strain, and tasks off our plate
- Be loyal to the vision or goal
- Expand our capacity to achieve goals

Counselors

If you live long enough, you'll find that you have blind spots—areas of your life where you don't see yourself clearly enough. In some instances, they are personal, other times social or professional. But you almost always need support to identify, correct, and recover from them.

This is where counselors come in. For the sake of accessibility and clarity, I want to distinguish between professional counselors for this section. I affirm and advocate for the need for mental health professionals, and I would encourage anyone reading this who feels that professional counseling would be beneficial to pursue it.

But when I use the word *counselors* in this context, I'm simply talking about people who can serve as a guide. What I've come to find is that some people guide us in and some people guide us out, but we all need guidance to thrive.

For David, this shows up after he becomes king, and his attention to his character and calling becomes blurred. Consequently, he finds himself committing infidelity with Bathsheba. He has lost his way as a leader and worshiper. The Lord sends Nathan, a prophet, to share with David a word of correction and conviction. But he also serves as a guide for David to see something inside that he's started to miss. To explore parts of his identity and character that have been overlooked due to the busyness of his schedule and burden of his assignment.

There are also times when we need someone to lead us out into the wilderness or to a new path. To give us wisdom on places they've already been and things they've already done. Perhaps it's for this reason the book of Proverbs goes to such great lengths to encourage us in this direction. Let's look at a few of them from the Amplified Version of the Bible:

> Where there is no [wise, intelligent] guidance, the
>   people fall [and go off course like a ship without a
>   helm],
> But in the abundance of [wise and godly] counselors
>   there is victory. (Prov. 11:14)

> Without consultation *and* wise advice, plans are
>   frustrated,
> But with many counselors they are established and
>   succeed. (Prov. 15:22)

> For by wise guidance you can wage your war,
> And in an abundance of [wise] counselors there is victory *and* safety. (Prov. 24:6)

What do we need counselors to do?

- Be unmoved by our success or charisma
- Speak truth no matter what
- Share wisdom and experiences
- Walk with us in hard or new seasons
- Review and advise on plans

At the end of each service at TLC, we extend an invitation for people to join our community of believers. This is what we call taking a next step to forge deeper relationships within the ecosystem of the community. Very often, we'll lead with these words: "A church isn't a bunch of perfect people, it's a bunch of imperfect people who've found a perfect God." People are imperfect—there's no denying that. But as the old African proverb says, "If you want to go fast, go alone. If you want to go far, go together."

If you take one thing away from this chapter, please take this: Find your people. For it's with people that you'll find power.

PART 3
THE GREAT UNKNOWN

NINE

No Guts, No Glory

"Ladies and gentlemen, welcome to the next phase of our journey. I'm your tour guide, Vernon Gordon, and I hope you have enjoyed your journey thus far. If you look to your right or to your left, you'll now see we're entering the wilderness. There's no turning back now. Welcome to the other side."

That's what I think the script should be for all honest people who've found the other side of their fears. We invite people to face their fears all the time, but what's on the other side of that familiar feeling and function? Promise? Not exactly.

We often consolidate our storylines to neatly fit the attention span of our generation. But rarely is there enough space in our social media post for the whole story. And table etiquette demands we not monopolize the conversation by delivering all the details. As such, we often see the start and finish but edit out the in-between.

The Great Unknown

There was a popular social media trend a few years ago that featured videos about fifteen seconds in length. You would see an initial image or footage of someone, and then it would say "Can we skip to the good part?" Immediately, the video would jump to the other side—to a life of fun, recovery, reconciliation, success, you name it.

But that's not how life actually works. We don't get to skip to the good part. That also doesn't mean we should stay in the bad part. The question I think we should be asking is: What's the middle part?

Now, I know what you're thinking. *Vernon, I've been with you for eight chapters, nine if I count the intro. But now you want to tell me at the onset of this last section of the book that this is not a silver bullet but an invitation to the unknown?* The answer is yes, but what I can 100 percent guarantee is that you'll never truly know what you could see if you don't brave the unknown. Or simply put: No guts, no glory.

Did you know that the phrase "No guts, no glory" was actually coined by American Air Force General Frederick Corbin Blesse? General Blesse was a highly decorated Air Force pilot who served in two tours during the Korean War and another two tours during the Vietnam War. He was revered by many as one of the most skilled pilots of his time. For perspective, he still ranks number six as a Jet Ace, and in the World Wide Air Force Fighter Weapons Meet in 1955, he flew an F-86 and won all six trophies offered for individual performance. That feat has never been equaled.

In 1955, he wrote a tactics manual that was used by the Air Force for twenty-five years. The title? *No Guts, No Glory.* Here's an excerpt from his preface:

> The greatest reward and the basis for all that is to follow, however, is the self-confidence the pilot feels in himself. As

this confidence grows, so does his enthusiasm. Enthusiasm increases interest, which in turn pays dividends in overall accomplishment. All of these qualities together add up to the one thing a training program must produce if the graduate pilots are to be successful in combat—aggressiveness. It is this pilot aggressiveness which we seek. Without it, all training is useless, for the individual pilot must have the desire to put into effect that which he has been taught.[1]

In this section, we move beyond a passive response to the world and seek to drive our lives forward. We firmly place both hands on the wheel and declare our confidence. Yes, even in the unknown. We are reminded that victory requires risk and accomplishment requires an aggressive pursuit of promise. A willingness to put into effect new lessons and language and to test our limits is a must. Simply put, the common denominator of calling is change.

We finally find our voice, our vision, and our victory, and then we enter the "What now?" phase of the journey. Over and over in Scripture we see this narrative play out as people face their fears.

Take, for example, the children of Israel. When they're first delivered from Egyptian captivity, they begin their journey with an unlikely plan of action by God. Exodus 13:17–18 says, "When Pharaoh let the people go, God did not lead them on the road through the Philistine country, though that was shorter. For God said, 'If they face war, they might change their minds and return to Egypt.' So God led the people around by the desert road toward the Red Sea."

Now, we who have the gift of hindsight love this idea of a route to the Red Sea. But for the people experiencing it, they were a bit confused. They gained freedom from captivity, but then God led them on a longer route by way of the desert, which could be the equivalent of a wilderness, with a final destination of what seems like an uncrossable Red Sea.

They weren't alone in trying to track God's steps. Later, Jesus would live in obscurity for thirty years before getting baptized, and what's next? The wilderness.

I love this passage because it contrasts our theological framework with Western Christianity—a belief system that hinges on God doing good, clear, profitable things. Matthew picks up the story of Jesus immediately following his baptism, when the skies open and the Lord says, "This is my Son, whom I love; with him I am well pleased" (Matt. 3:17). Then it says, "Then Jesus was led by the Spirit into the wilderness to be tempted by the devil" (4:1).

Well, I didn't see that coming. How could the Spirit of God lead Jesus into the wilderness to be tempted? Never mind that God just said he was proud of him. This is one of the most baffling series of events in Scripture. It suggests to us that there are times when following God's plan won't lead you to comfort but to confusion and confrontation.

Now, I don't want you to think the wilderness always looks like being lost or in lack. Sometimes it's just being lost in leadership or being lost in success.

Jesus was lost because he was preparing, Moses and the Israelites were lost because of protection, Jonah was lost because of redirection, Ruth was lost because of loyalty. All were experiencing the other side of following their future beyond their fears. And all learned a valuable lesson in the process.

God never wastes a wilderness. He refines, reveals, restores, and revives in the unknown.

In the movie *Frozen*, Elsa is a queen who has been kept in hiding for most of her life because of her power to control elements related to the cold. At a young age, unaware of how to control her power, she accidentally hurt her younger sister

Anna, resulting in a family decision to keep the two apart. Not only did the two remain apart, but their parents closed the gates of their castle to shield Elsa from exposure to the outside world. Following the untimely loss of their parents, Elsa is next in line to lead the kingdom, resulting in her need to mask her powers while in front of others. During her coronation, she attempts to do this but is unsuccessful and ends up freezing the entire kingdom, causing her to flee the castle and head into the wilderness.

As she treks through the uncharted, snowy land, for the first time she's free to explore her powers. In a matter of minutes, you see a transformation in Elsa as she discovers just how powerful she really can be. From nothing she creates structures, snow giants, and more. It's from this scene we get the song "Let It Go."

My synopsis? The invitation into the unfamiliar was always the prerequisite to her maximized potential. Without it, she would never have had the space to fully discover just how strong she could be. The unknown began as a place of escape but turned into a place of evolution.

The same is true for our lives. Fear's first assignment is not pain or prevention but perspective. It causes us to reframe our perception of our own potential and power. To see ourselves as grasshoppers when we're the giant. To disconnect from our Creator and shrink ourselves into our culture.

However, fear has a flaw. It is neutral. It is not strong or weak. It is not smart or stupid. It's simply a checkpoint, a mile marker on the race we run. Once I embrace that, the unknown doesn't scare me as much. Because while it may introduce a new type of fear, I've seen fear before. It doesn't evolve; it simply shows up. I then choose how big or how small to make it in my life. I choose how loud or how quiet to make it in my heart. I can adjust the volume whenever I take control.

So, step into the unknown, the next, the future. Remember: No guts, no glory.

■ ■ ■

In the late 1800s, the US Army on the frontier recruited a group of Black Seminole Scouts to help them protect routes, fulfill missions, and navigate the terrain. Many of these soldiers were African Americans who had successfully escaped slavery. They found a home in Florida and intermarried with the Seminoles, allowing them to settle in the traditions and safety of that community.

Once recruited, they became an essential part of the military strategy. It is said that they saw combat in extremely rugged conditions on both sides of the border. Out of twenty-six expeditions, the scouts engaged in twelve battles without losing a single man in combat. As a unit, they gained a reputation of dedication and bravery as they navigated not only the bludgeons of war but racial prejudice from within their own military camps. Stationed continuously on the frontier from the 1860s to the 1890s, they played a major role in the settlement of the American West.

The scouts were praised for their abilities, but I think the true power of their story is in their adaptability. From slavery to integration with the Seminole community. From scouts to soldiers. They figured out a way in every territory to thrive. The environment didn't dictate their effectiveness.

At the heart of all three hundred plus "fear nots" by God in the Bible is a simple truth: There was a reason to fear. A war to win, a risk revealed, a danger discovered, or a pressure presented that was legitimate and worthy of concern. And yet, God's call was "Do not be afraid." Now, at first glance, we could see this as insensitive and be downright disillusioned by his response.

However, there's often an overlooked principle at play. A strategy unseen on the surface. Which is why we can't forget this simple truth:

Being lost is very different from being led.

Jesus was led by the Spirit into the wilderness. Moses was led on the longer route toward the Red Sea. I was led to leave a stable Baptist church and plant a church. You might be led to do something that seems unclear or unknown. My hope is that you trust me when I say it's always worth it.

So, how do we brave new territory as we find the other side of fear? Here are three key principles to navigating the unknown, borrowed from one of the greatest military victories of all time, the Battle of Jericho (Josh. 5:13–6:27). If the names Joshua or Jericho don't stand out to you, what may be more familiar is the story of an army shouting and walls coming down. This military victory marks a pivotal moment in the lives of their new leader Joshua and of their community as the first victory in the promised land, and it signals to all their upcoming opponents that God is with them.

So, how'd they do it? And what is there to learn?

Principle 1: Keep It Simple

You've probably heard it said that if you fail to plan, you plan to fail. New seasons require new plans. But as you're building a personal plan, resist the temptation to drift to complexity.

I played high school basketball, and our coach was a fundamentals guy. Coach Leroy Ricks, who was also a deacon at his church, was a no-nonsense leader focused on endurance, passing, dribbling, and shooting. If we got the fundamentals right, we were going to be good.

What I'm sure made his job much more difficult was that at that time, basketball was being influenced by more than the fundamentals. The AND1 basketball movement was taking over the sports scene, and it represented what every kid wanted to be. It influenced how we all were dribbling, passing, shooting, even dressing. Please don't ask to see pictures; it wasn't pretty.

But Coach Leroy Ricks was clear: Save all that for time with your friends. Here, on my court, it's about KISS: Keep it simple, stupid. That's where our success would be found. In simple moves, simple plays, and simple plans.

I love looking at the leadership of Joshua in Canaan. Let's look at this from his point of view, shall we? They have been waiting for forty years to get to this land. Everyone is eager, optimistic, and energized. They cross over, and the first thing they have to do is fight to occupy the land.

It's also relevant to note that Joshua is building this plan as a new leader recently charged with this assignment after a beloved leader named Moses has died. In simple terms: Don't screw this up, man.

So, what does he do?

1. Prays and invites God into the planning
2. Learns from the lessons of the past by sending two scouts instead of twelve like his predecessor
3. Communicates a clear plan that can be repeated and retained

Make no mistake about it, the plan he receives from God isn't just strange now to us, but it would have been strange to them as well. Strange but simple. Here's the plan that he received from God: Walk around the wall every day, don't talk, and after seven days, shout.

I imagine there were a bunch of people who were like, "Is that it?" Yep, that's it. But it's simple. Everybody can share it, take it on the go, and remember it.

As you're making your next plan, I'd encourage you to do the same. What I've found time and time again is that most of God's plans aren't complicated. They're simple. Simple doesn't always mean easy, but they always equal success if you follow them.

Principle 2: Secure Support

After you build a plan, you cannot escape the need to find your allies. We talked about this in the preceding chapter. You need people, and people need you. This doesn't always mean we have to eliminate friends and partners from the previous season, but it almost always requires us to expand on our relationships.

A few questions you should ask are:

1. Who understands the land (this can be a metaphor for an industry, field, sector, environment, community, etc.) we're headed into and can provide counsel?
2. Who has shown themself to be a person of peace? One who is here to open their door, table, network, or schedule for us to learn?
3. Who could benefit from what we have to offer as well? Is there a mutual benefit in this strategic relationship?

These probing questions can be a guide to identifying the right allies for this territory you're entering on the other side of fear. How does Joshua model this for us?

The Bible reveals to us in Joshua 2 a strategic story that is vital to the victory over Jericho. When the spies are sent out, they are protected by a prostitute named Rahab. She not only allows the spies into her home but hides them when they are discovered and throws Jericho's army off their tracks for three days.

At the conclusion of this gesture, they make an agreement to spare her life and the lives of her family upon their conquering of the land. But there's a small piece of information that military historians believe is overlooked in this story. If you'd allow me, I want to explore this at length, and it might ruffle some theological conservatism feathers in the process, but stick with me. The story reads, "So she let them down by a rope through the window, for the house she lived in was part of the city wall. . . . Now the men had said to her, 'This oath you made us swear will not be binding on us unless, when we enter the land, you have tied this scarlet cord in the window through which you let us down'" (vv. 15, 17–18).

Some military strategists and theologians think the placement of Rahab's house is the primary reason she was chosen for partnership. This placement allowed for an escape to safety by the spies as they were lowered down by a rope from the window. The question emerges, What if the same rope that allowed a safe exit could allow for a safe entry?

This would then add to the attention we should give to their requested oath—that when they enter the land, the same cord that she let them down with should be hanging from the window. What if the same cord that let them down was also used to let them up?

If we take this bit of information and combine it with the strategy God gave to Joshua, we see a new possibility. As they walked around the wall once a day for seven days, they were instructed to be quiet. What if their silence was less about simple discipline and more about simple strategy? This allows members of their army to enter on the scarlet rope to reach safety within the walls.

Furthermore, after a significant group had made safe entry up the city wall on the cord that was hanging from the window, the shout was then a signal to those inside to begin the attack from the inside out.

In this theory, Jericho's walls falling down is less about the physical falling of the walls and more of a military metaphor—that the wall that could not be defeated "fell" as a result of a simple strategy and the right support from the inside.

Now, this is not to shake your faith, whether you believe the wall came down physically or metaphorically. There is no denying the support of Rahab was essential to the strategy of God and the plans of Joshua.

Securing the right support can be the key you're looking for as you take new ground and overcome new fears.

Principle 3: Don't Stray from the Strategy

Okay, Bible trivia time: How many times did they march around Jericho?

If you said thirteen, you're correct. If you said seven, you're wrong. This is one of my favorite Bible trivia questions from the time I was a youth pastor until now. Most of us say seven because they marched around for seven days.

But if we look closely, Joshua's instructions are as follows:

> "March around the city once with all the armed men. Do this for six days. Have seven priests carry trumpets of rams' horns in front of the ark. On the seventh day, march around the city seven times, with the priests blowing the trumpets. When you hear them sound a long blast on the trumpets, have the

whole army give a loud shout; then the wall of the city will collapse and the army will go up, everyone straight in." . . .

But Joshua had commanded the army, "Do not give a war cry, do not raise your voices, do not say a word until the day I tell you to shout. Then shout!" (Josh. 6:3–5, 10)

They were to walk around the city once a day for six days then seven times on the seventh day for a total of thirteen laps around the wall.

Now, I'm only talking about myself here, but walking around something in a circle, quietly, and every day with no action? I would have been the weak link. I would've been impatient, and certainly the "no talking" part would have canceled me out. And yet, the key to their success is not improvisation, it's staying with the strategy.

So often what fear instigates is pressure to change the plans. Redo everything. Impulsively go in a different direction. We may call it many things, but at its root, fear is the great disruptor of faithfulness. We must be faithful not only to God but also to his instruction, strategy, and plan.

It might feel like you're just walking. You're not doing anything. You're wasting your time. But when you have a strategy, don't stray. Find your footing and follow the plan. This will bring life, leadership, equity, and results.

So, welcome: You're on the other side now. Fear can't hold you anymore. Ready to learn more about the other side? Let's keep going.

TEN

Higher Ground

"Let's go hiking!" they said. I was reluctant and honestly unsure of what I was getting myself into. But I'm not one to turn down a challenge, so I said, "Let's do it." And off we went to conquer the mountain.

It would probably be good to offer some background as to how this journey came to be. As I mentioned earlier, in 2018, I was invited to be a part of a leadership cohort called Uptick. As I became closer with my fellow participants, we began sharing our life experiences. Our group represented many different ethnicities, and quite naturally, our conversation began to cover cultural exposure as well, including activities we saw growing up, family norms, and the difference between a barbecue and a cookout (it was very important information being shared here).

Organically, the conversation progressed to things we had never ventured to do. One of the guys I became close with was from Texas and could be considered a classic adventurer. He ran the outdoor adventure recreation for Baylor University, had backpacked across states for days, and had hiked many a mountain. He was the prototypical American guy. He was built for the good ole outdoors and male traditions. He was also one of the kindest and most insightful human beings I had ever met and had a knack for inspiring exploration in me for things I had never consumed and experiences I had never considered.

As for me, I grew up in a traditional Black community. Which means hiking was not on the weekend itinerary, ever. So, he recommended to the group that we do just that with the free time we had in the schedule. Admittedly, I was nervous. But the competitor in me—and, yes, maybe even my pride—wouldn't allow me to say no. Not only had I never been hiking before but I also had a total knee replacement that I'd never put to the test like this. Add to that the fact that I was going with people I'd just met two months ago. It seemed like a recipe for embarrassment and disaster. Nonetheless, we took off. With every twist and turn, rock and meadow, I was enamored with the beauty of God's creation and the peace that nature provided. I felt physically challenged but spiritually alive. We took several breaks on the way up, so it took us hours to reach the top, but when we did, we arrived at a view that, while cliché, was breathtaking. The journey to the view was challenging, tedious, and tiring, pushing my body to the limit, but the reward was the view. Things were so much clearer at the top.

Fear has a way of stopping us before we ever get started. As we talked about earlier, it shows up in many forms but each with the same assignment: to talk us out of taking the next step. In our humanity, we tend to focus our line of sight on what was lost and the risk of the unknown. Or even worse, we allow the visibility of the present to obstruct the vision of our future. However, fear and worry do not have to be the place of our imprisonment. We can reclaim and redeem our vision for our future if we take the journey to higher heights.

For this to occur, our eyes cannot be limited to screens and struggle; instead, we must look toward something greater, something higher. And the harsh truth is this: If you don't change what you see, you can't change what you start. So, I want to encourage you to stop focusing on outcomes and start focusing on outlooks. You can't control everywhere you'll end up. You can control what you're looking at on the way there.

In fairness, the word *outlook* is thrown around a lot, but I want to park here for a moment so you can know what I mean when I say *outlook*. By definition, an outlook is a person's point of view or general attitude toward life or a place from which a view is possible; a vantage point. When you think about it, it's a powerful concept that we have both the ability and choice to adjust our attitude toward life even when we can't control the experience. If you haven't heard it before, attitude is everything.

Why does this matter? Because we live in a culture that is obsessed with maximized potential of gifts, profits, platforms, and networks. And yet I've come to find that potential is a great pursuit but isn't the source of its own power. Potential is a rocket with no fuel. It sits idle without the right attitude. Attitude and outlook are the fuel to a successful launch into new orbits of living.

How we see ourselves, our experiences, and others informs how we act, respond, and believe. Ultimately, attitude determines how far we can move beyond our immediate existence. When most people think of attitude, we minimize it to the coworker whose commentary we don't like or superficial expressions of passion, culture, and entertainment. However, attitude plays a vital role in our everyday lives. All of us must account for it to maintain control of our character and potential. A change in attitude always precedes a change in altitude.

For example, a moment of professional disappointment can be seen as an opportunity to grow or a reason to hide in shame. A spouse's continued inability to meet expectations can be seen as an act of offense or an opportunity for emotional intimacy and vulnerability. A lost game can be the demise of a team's focus or the catalyst to their season's motivation. In each of these scenarios, the outcome is determined by the outlook.

How we see a situation determines how we direct our emotions and actions toward it. Does a professional setback or failure drive us to mentorship or insecurity? Does marriage turbulence turn into a season of greater clarity and emotional openness or a sea of silent resentment? Does the team learn from their mistakes and mobilize around a shared goal, or do they play the blame game and never recover? Outlook is the key. When we choose to maintain the right outlook, even in difficult seasons, we move closer and closer to the views that the other side of struggle always provides.

■ ■ ■

As mentioned earlier, it wasn't that long ago that I went on my first hike. The benefit at the time was companionship from those who had walked the path before. Their experience and encouragement made the journey all the more possible. At each turn, they pointed out the unique greenery around us, ways to conserve energy, and strategies for making good time. At the conclusion of the journey, I saw the beauty of a broad landscape of endless earth. I was hooked and had an appetite to experience that feeling again. A few short weeks later, I found myself at a conference with a hiking trail a few short miles away, so I invited two of my friends to join me. Both of them had little to no experience hiking, but I figured, how hard could it be?

At the onset of the journey, it seemed that this would be a breeze, but only a few moments later, we knew we had made a grave mistake. We weren't dressed in the right attire, hadn't brought any water or fueling snacks, and had no idea what was around us and what risk we might be in. We were on our own.

All the more concerning, I was serving as our guide because although I only had one hike under my belt, I was the most experienced hiker in our group. The journey was rough, unpredictable, and downright dangerous at times. Yet, once we got to the top, all was forgotten. We were once again celebrating overcoming the mountain and the beauty of new views.

Hiking those mountains got me thinking. How many mountains are we not climbing? How many paths are we not taking? How many views will we never arrive at, simply because we've allowed our attitude and outlook to focus on unknowns, not on possibilities and potential?

Becoming brave doesn't begin with having all the answers or all the experience. We took the journey that day full of naivety. Yet, we were driven by hope and the possibility of memories in the making. Once we arrived at higher ground, all the challenges of the journey were worth it. Developing a healthy outlook is hard work, but you've got to start somewhere, like with all things. And somewhere, well, that always begins with a look in the mirror.

In James, we find the words, "Do not merely listen to the word, and so deceive yourselves. Do what it says. Anyone who listens to the word but does not do what it says is like someone who looks at his face in a mirror and, after looking at himself, goes away and immediately forgets what he looks like" (1:22–24).

James is writing to us from generations past with a warning. The power to receive is easy; the power to retain is what takes work. Inspiration, encouragement, and vision are all easy to receive and welcome at the start of any journey. But if we only listen and don't do something with them, well, that's like a person who forgets what they look like. Let's remember who we've been called to be and go after it.

Now, to be fair, some barriers work against us taking ownership of our outlook. Our news, entertainment, and social media are doing their part to influence our thoughts, opinions, and actions. Add to that our own memories that, if we allow them to, can restrict us from seeing beautiful horizons and hopes. Sometimes it's our families' and friends' limited exposure and faith that crowd our conversations. It can be our insecurities and complacency that can stand in the way.

Ultimately, our attitude toward a season or situation is generally the result of personal preferences, past experiences, or environmental influences. Here are a few guiding thoughts to overcome each mountain that stands in the way of you taking ownership of your outlook.

Take the first step. Our personal preferences play a huge role in minimizing our potential views in life. Especially in today's society, the power of choice is our greatest advancement and our greatest kryptonite. We prefer it faster, so we pay extra for expedited arrival. We prefer it closer, so we google locations near us. We prefer it to be easier, so we abandon commitments whenever we like. We prefer it be with a certain group of people, so we avoid building any new or emerging community around us. We prefer it to be with this salary, so we choose money over fulfillment. The list goes on and on. In a society where passion is often predicated on profit or preference, we must fight for the courage to live beyond preferential practices.

Higher ground is attainable, but not without effort and (a big word here) inconvenience. I've often found that my outlook changes while walking, not while waiting. One thing was consistent in the two hikes I mentioned earlier: My mindset changed in the process, not in the principle. That is to say, it wasn't until I took one step forward, and then the next, and then the next, that my confidence and excitement evolved. With each of those experiences, I was nervous and felt unprepared at the start. However, I didn't allow my personal preferences to rob me of the eventual peak. I pushed myself. It was only when I exhausted my perceived potential that I could have a new perspective revealed. Higher ground is waiting for those who can push beyond their personal preferences. And where there's higher ground, there's a different vantage point.

The past is a guide, not a god. Past experiences can be valuable in decision-making, motivation, and resilience, particularly in seasons where setbacks and disappointment are present. It's essential to learn from our past and appropriately apply the lessons it provides. However, if given unhealthy attention, it can plant significant roadblocks in our progress. In this scenario, our failures become a place that defines us and doesn't develop us. We must resist this at all costs. It is possible to remember the past and not react to it. When we respond to the past as if it's the present, we limit our ability to see clearly what gifts the present offers. We misread relationships, partnerships, opportunities, disappointments, and difficulties. We automatically filter the present through the past and revert to a default response. We could unfairly create walls where we should build bridges, we could erect idols where we should have only had seasonal celebrations, or we could set up cities where we should have only set up camp. The past is not the problem; the way we process it is. It can be a problem or a partner; you must decide.

Recently, I was playing golf with a group of friends, and we decided to play a scramble. This type of golf simply means you are on a two- or four-person team where each person hits the ball, and after each shot, you get to decide which of the best shots you will play. With great humility, I must admit we didn't use many of my shots that day. My teammates were much more experienced golfers than I, and let's just say I was there primarily for moral support. However, whenever we arrived on the greens, it was time to putt. And that is something I can do fairly well. When putting in a scramble, the first person on the team is generally trying to give their teammate a good "read" on the ball. Where is it breaking, what's the speed of the greens and the general path toward the hole? You might've heard the saying "Give me a good read." If I wanted to turn this into a catchy phrase, I'd say, "Give me a read so I can succeed." As corny as that sounds, it means that each attempt serves to further your chances at finding the best path to success.

In the same way, our past should not lead us, but it can give us a good read. It can be a source that informs wiser decision-making, sober judgment, and progressive thinking. Our past can be a building block for our future, but it should never be the builder. It has its place in the foundation but also has limitations on what it can offer the broader architecture of your life. Your commitment to properly placing your past in the framework of conversations, aspirations, and challenging seasons will be essential to your future.

Build, don't borrow. The battle for the mind is not a coming war; it is here. With every click, swipe, share, and new feature on our devices, our access to any and all information is at an all-time high. And as algorithms seek to fulfill their assignment to attract our eyes and ears, it's safe to say ownership of thought is the greatest commodity we can carry. Our cultural climate doesn't exactly bend toward thought ownership as much as we might think. Borrowed thoughts are the recipe for most conversations in our day and age.

According to a 2021 study by the Pew Research Center:

> 60 percent of all adults in the United States said they often get their news on a smartphone, and 53 percent sometimes or often get their news from social media.
>
> 40 percent said they often get their news from various television outlets.[1]

Now, I'm not saying we should burn our smartphones and take our televisions to the dump. However, when credibility and media aren't necessarily mutually inclusive, we must wisely choose our convictions and perspectives. The age-old truth to stand for something or fall for anything still rings true, but it takes more effort and energy than ever to own that truth with sober and sound judgment. Unfortunately, it's not just the media that's after our attitude and outlook. It's a myriad of environmental and social influences. It's network and neighborhood and other times friendships and family. Our environment plays a crucial role in our capacity to grow, cultivate, and conceive new outlooks.

Have you ever heard of the koi fish? It's a cold-water fish that primarily lives in Asia and central Europe. They are known for their unique color variations and are often displayed in decorative water features. But that's not the only thing that makes the koi interesting. In one study, researchers took a group of koi and placed some in a fish tank, others in a pond, and others in a lake. The results? The koi confined to the boundaries of a fish tank only grew to four inches. The koi allowed to grow in the pond grew to eighteen inches. And the koi that lived in the lake grew to forty-two inches.² The principle speaks for itself; the environment has an impact on growth. We must keep this principle in mind as we consider what it means to expand our outlook.

Maybe you're asking, What about environments that are not so easily modified? How do you manage workplace or neighborhood realities? What do you do for the people and places you can't avoid or abandon? The truth is we can't change some environments, so we must manage them. To own your thoughts, you must first see yourself as the owner of your life.

This outlook is crucial to grasp. Taking ownership of your thoughts and emotions will often require taking ownership of your environments. The danger of not doing so is burying our minds in borrowed ideas, which ultimately leads to a lack of fulfillment for and faithfulness to our future selves.

Here's how Paul talks about it in Romans 12: "And so, dear brothers and sisters, I plead with you to give your bodies to God because of all he has done for you. Let them be a living and holy sacrifice—the kind he will find acceptable. This is truly the way to worship him. Don't copy the behavior and customs of this world, but let God transform you into a new person by changing the way you think. Then you will learn to know God's will for you, which is good and pleasing and perfect" (vv. 1–2 NLT).

What is Paul trying to tell us? That if we're not careful, we can borrow behaviors and beliefs that are inconsistent with God's will for our lives. But what he desires is that we have the bravery to break out of social and environmental prisons to find a life of authenticity and power. To recognize that there's more to see and do and become if only we resist the urge to borrow and accept the responsibility to build.

Recently, my wife and I moved into a new home. One notable aspect of our backyard was the extensive greenery and gardens planted by the previous owners. Everything from rich soil to strawberries, roses, and fresh vegetables filled our backyard landscape. It's important to note that none of this was a part of the original landscaping. Our neighbors shared with us that our predecessors had green thumbs and were visionary landscapers. They told us that the vision we see today resulted from their digging, developing, and cultivating the land over the years to be conducive to fruitfulness. They found spaces within their inherited environment where soil could be seeded, plants could be properly exposed to sunlight, and fruit could receive adequate moisture. They could have looked out over the land and determined that what existed upon arrival was a final and fixed product. Honestly, that is most certainly what I would have done because I have no green thumb whatsoever. Instead, they saw a picture of possibility and set out to alter the environment to ensure growth was attainable. They modified the house and the environment surrounding it according to their preferred future, not their inherited one.

We must do likewise! We must all choose to dig, develop, and cultivate the landscape we receive. We may inherit the environment, but that doesn't mean we can't steward it toward fruitfulness. For some of us, this will look like limiting the amount of time we are present in certain environments, reducing the length of certain conversations, or reimagining our interactions within specific spaces. For others, it will look like placing a time limit on calls, scheduling our phones to go on "Do Not Disturb" mode at a particular time of day, and increasing our intake of affirming or healthy content. All of these choices act as a measure of balance for what we consume beyond our control. Do whatever it takes, dig, develop, and cultivate places, spaces, and time for the types of growth you desire. Don't simply borrow ideas and ideologies, but build your thoughts and your life on solid foundations.

The journey to higher ground is waiting for us all. Take your first step, learn from the past, and build toward your future. What's awaiting is a beautiful view, a conquered mountain, a fruitful lot, and a new way of thinking. Be brave, be bold, be new.

ELEVEN

Inside Out

Let's settle this once and for all. *Inside Out* is not a kids' movie. It's a movie that everybody should see.

Now, if you're one of those people who doesn't want someone to tell them what happened in a movie, avert your eyes. For everyone else, let's keep reading.

In 2015, Pixar released an animated movie called *Inside Out*. The film highlighted the emotions of a young girl, Riley, and her parents—in particular, how their "inner conversations" between their emotions showed up in their outward actions. Five primary emotions were vying for control of Riley's attitude, behavior, and ultimately her quality of life: Fear, Anger, Sadness, Disgust, and Joy.

As the film goes on, Joy and Sadness get lost and have to search for a way back to the seat of influence over Riley's character. At the onset of this movie, Joy was frustrated with the other emotions placed in Riley's life, not understanding why they were necessary. In particular, she saw no value in the presence of Sadness. It was only because of their need to work together to return that she learned something unexpected: All of the emotions were needed to make Riley healthy and whole. Most importantly, they discovered that Joy would not be as valued without the experience of all the other emotions.

In the second installment of this film, released in 2024, four new emotions emerge as Riley matures: Anxiety, Ennui, Embarrassment, and Envy. Throughout the film, there is another battle for control, and what becomes apparent by the end is that every emotion assumes they're helping. In one powerful moment, Anxiety is losing control, and it's manifested as Riley having a panic attack. Joy finally appears and gently shares with Anxiety that she has to let go. And yet again, viewers are reminded of the way our emotions work together to help ground our existence.

While this animated film was undoubtedly made about children, I have shared it with countless adults. Very few films have been as impactful and clear as the *Inside Out* movies in communicating the powerful role emotions play in all our lives. While emotions are always there, there is no time when they are louder than in seasons of fear and worry. They scream at our insecurities, broadcast our failures, and fan the flames of our fatigue. It seems like joy moves out in these moments.

But what if I told you your emotions don't have to get the best of you? What if there was a way not to avoid them but to manage them for the sake of your strength and the purity of shaping your future?

Here's the big idea: Either you manage your emotions or your emotions will manage you.

That's the choice. Because emotions are always along for the ride. As a matter of fact, I worry about a person who is emotionless. Apathy is no way to go through life. The presence of joy and pain, hope and sadness, victory and defeat, is essential to our character formation.

Managing emotions sounds simple enough, but one of the challenges we all face in our culture is that life comes at us fast. And getting control of what's happening within may require us to slow down and even start over at times. But don't fret; sometimes starting over means the chance to start stronger. I'd go so far as to say starting over is an oversimplification of what's potentially occurring in our life. Let me explain what I mean.

Every major league sport has an offseason. The previous season is done, and the athletes await the new season. During the playing season, athletes have to consistently be "on," always ready for game day. But the offseason is when they "work on" their strength, speed, and strategies. The offseason makes them better.

I once asked an NFL coach who had experienced sustained success how he motivates his team year after year to play with the same passion and commitment to excellence. His answer was simple: "I tell them, 'Last season was last season, nobody cares, we're back to square one.'" Very inspirational, I know!

However, as our conversation continued, I realized that it didn't mean all their work in the previous season was without reward. They had built principles, strength, experience, confidence, and chemistry in the last season. But they trained for more power, wisdom, and morale in the offseason.

What makes you ready for a new season is how you handle an offseason.

The problem is life doesn't give us an offseason. You don't get to tell your supervisor that you need three weeks off so you can perform better. You don't get to tell people relying on you to meet deadlines to lower their expectations because you're not in season. You certainly don't get to tell your kids or your spouse, "Hey, for the next thirty days, I'm going to be in an offseason, just so y'all know." Try it and let me know how that works. An offseason is not the abandonment of responsibility and presence but rather the intentional space created to heal, stretch, and grow so that we can show up better in every season.

With the proper perspective, we can bring both truth and the right attitude to our emotions. Emotions are not our enemies; they are our guides. They are not to be neglected but noticed, named, and nurtured. Only when we possess the discipline to be constructed by them and not controlled by them will we find the best version of ourselves.

Even more, we must resist the notion that a solid and meaningful life is one lived without struggle and disappointment. Under those metrics, Martin Luther King Jr. didn't have a meaningful life. Harriet Tubman didn't have a meaningful life. One could even say Jesus didn't have a meaningful life. Certainly not.

Meaning is not derived from the absence of emotions and hardship but rather from the stewardship of them into something more significant and of service to our world. T. K. Coleman writes, "Inner freedom is less about feeling good and more about learning to develop a healthy and harmonious relationship with the variety of emotional states you're likely to occupy over the course of a lifetime."[1]

Emotions will always be present; what we do with them is the choice that frames our futures. In all of this, there is a simple truth I'll say again. Either you manage your emotions or your emotions will manage you. And all too often, we allow emotions to speak for us, think for us, relate for us, decide for us, and respond for us. However, there is a better way and a healthier way.

It starts with better management of our environments. Every environment is an energy source or energy assassin. When we don't have the necessary emotional energy, we struggle to fight compromising thoughts and emotions. Feelings are normal. Feelings mixed with fatigue are a dangerous combination. Under these conditions, we yield to behaviors and beliefs that are inconsistent with our preferred future. We find ourselves sucked into fear and worry more frequently. When facing fear, we can't afford to be casual about the environments we choose to dwell in. Here are some good questions to ask yourself when managing your environments:

Where do I feel drained the most?
What places/people energize me?
Where are my reservoirs of joy?
How does my rhythm of life contribute to my emotional well-being?
Is there someone who always makes me feel stronger when I leave their presence?
Where does my soul feel at rest?

Until we learn to manage our environments, we'll never see where our energy gets lost and where it can be fueled to help us overcome. It's also my sincere hope that you see these questions as a continuation of a conversation that is threaded throughout this book.

Most people know of John 11 because it contains the shortest verse in the Bible: "Jesus wept" (v. 35). But the story around this incident is insightful and instructive for our understanding of emotions.

One of Jesus's best friends, Lazarus, has died. His sisters, Mary and Martha, are disappointed in Jesus because they sent word to him days ago to come and help their brother, and Jesus didn't come in time. When you take the time to read the passage, notice who Mary and Martha are in the company of when Jesus arrives: mourners (v. 19). People whose job it is to keep them crying. It wasn't that the mourners were bad people, but they weren't helping them move beyond their emotions; they were helping them sit in them. Don't get me wrong; as I said earlier, all emotions are necessary, but they are a place you visit, not a place you live in.

Could it be that some of our weakest moments are the result of choosing the wrong company? Don't mistake my thought here. Empathy should be appreciated, and those who have the gift of expressing it are to be valued. But don't allow empathy to be the only value. It must be coupled with encouragement and empowerment. The environment can add or subtract. Manage it well.

Additionally, we must manage our expectations. If we're honest, most of our frustration with people, life, and even God comes from experiences where expectations are not met. This is heightened in a world of exposed failures all around us. We can see others fly and fall, and even if it's not our story, the fear that it could be is enough to keep us grounded.

One of the things we share in our premarital classes is a simple formula for life: The space between expectation and reality is the measure of your disappointment. In other words, however large the gap between what you expected and what you see is how much disappointment, frustration, agitation, irritation, and anger you'll feel in your heart.

We have to fight to close that gap between expectation and reality. Otherwise, we leave ourselves vulnerable for fear, anxiety, and worry to set up camp in our minds and hearts without invitation.

Let's consider that "Jesus wept" Scripture again for a moment. Most people would argue that Jesus wept because he was sad, but that's inconsistent with Jesus's commentary. Jesus is weeping because he's irritated. Read it for yourself. Before he arrives, he says Lazarus will live; he's only sleeping. However, upon arrival, he's met with three different expressions of disappointment by Martha, Mary, and the people gathered. Here's the CliffsNotes version: "Jesus, you didn't meet our expectations." What happened?

Their present emotions overwhelmed their greater truth. Never lose your grip on the truth over your life. You are not a failure because you failed. You are not unworthy because you've been unsuccessful. You are not unloved because you are imperfect. You are worthy; you are loved; you are called to great things beyond what you feel, see, and hear.

Last, management of our expressions is crucial. There is no greater waste of strength than fighting battles that don't deserve attention. The truth is many battles can be fought that move our feelings but don't move us forward.

We feel vindicated but still feel visionless. We feel justified but also jaded. We feel worthy but also winded. Energy was used to move the needle on our feelings but not our future.

Emotions have a unique way of making us more expressive, particularly in response to a perceived challenge. Sometimes, that battle is in our minds, and we project emotions and power struggles onto ourselves. Other times, the battle is with those beyond us, real or perceived, who we believe we have to overcome in pursuit of our future. It's what we say and what we don't say that consumes us. The caution here is simple: Don't let your emotions make an enemy that may not exist.

■ ■ ■

In her book *Daring Greatly*, Brené Brown says,

Vulnerability is not knowing victory or defeat, it's understanding the necessity of both; it's engaging. It's being all in. When we consider the role emotions play in our lives, we minimize them to inconveniences, not necessities. To be all-in on life is to accept the beauty and blunt force of emotions. To fully live, we must fully feel. For a long time, I looked at my emotions as my weakness. But time would tell a different story. What we do with our emotions is by far the most vital discipline we could have in life. More important than any diet for our bodies or mind, emotions are the diet of the soul. What we feed determines the health of our whole being.[2]

It is for this reason that taking ownership of our emotions is so paramount. Emotional ownership is the practice and protection of personal peace aligned with God's promise for our lives. We see this promise clearly in John 14:25–27: "I am telling you these things now while I am still with you. But when the Father sends the Advocate as my representative—that is, the Holy Spirit—he will teach you everything and will remind you of everything I have told you. I am leaving you with a gift—peace of mind and heart. And the peace I give is a gift the world cannot give. So don't be troubled or afraid" (NLT).

Have you ever bumped into a gift that you forgot you had? Stumbled upon a present that, for the life of you, you couldn't remember where you got it? The card with the money in it or that free pass? Isn't it interesting that sometimes the indiscriminate investment was hiding in the human crevice of carelessness? It illuminates the issue of irresponsibility that often shows up in our life. Jesus says in the passage that we have been given a gift—peace of mind and heart. In today's world, where emotions are more influential than ever before, what a gift this would be to find.

What worries me is that most of us have forfeited emotional ownership, settling by outsourcing our emotions to outlets, opinions, and obstacles. Over time, if unaddressed, this will affect the fruit of our lives and hearts. When our lives face fear, it opens the door for emotional attacks. But it also opens the door for emotional alignment.

There was a young woman named Dominique Stevens in our congregation for the last several years. Dominique had a rare disease that compromised many of her major organs and her quality of life. In her thirties, she found herself unable to work, needing a wheelchair for mobility, and requiring full-time care from her family. And yet, every Sunday she could physically attend, she would find her way into our building. A smile on her face, hugs ready to be handed out, hands lifted during the music, and heart open to sharing encouragement with everyone she met. She passed away in 2021, and her funeral was full of people sharing how she encouraged them throughout the latter part of her life. The only obvious question for any reasonable person to ask is, How? She had every reason to be upset, discontented, and overtaken by circumstance, and yet she served as an encourager to so many. She took ownership of her emotions, never allowing her condition to compromise her character.

Earlier in this chapter, we highlighted how to manage our emotions. Now, let's quickly look at three primary responses to an emotional attack that all lead to emotional alignment.

You Cannot Fix Everything You Feel

The first is more of a personal permission, a grace even, that I hope you would extend to yourself. A simple reminder that

I've had to tell myself repeatedly over the last thirty-seven years. You cannot fix everything you feel.

The level of exposure we've had to tragedy is unprecedented and unseen in any previous generation. The temptation to be the hero in every story is not only unrealistic, but it leads us down a path of profound dissatisfaction with life and joy. We must reconcile the fact that although the emergence of feelings is inevitable with access to so much information through phones, articles, tabloids, and algorithms, we cannot possibly solve everything we see. We can no doubt be allies, refuse to be willfully ignorant, and act when necessary. However, we must also recognize our limitations and manage our guilt so that we can remain healthy enough to stay strong and brave for generations to come.

Tame Your Imagination

Imagination in and of itself is not a bad thing at all. But in seasons of emotional attack, it can be the weapon that works against our strength and personal success. Imagination is a gift to the disciplined, but it's a trap to the weak. Our ability to discern the difference between an imagination running wild and an imagination running well is crucial.

My kids are eleven and nine years old and have active imaginations. They can entertain themselves for hours creating characters, making forts, and dreaming up possibilities. As a creative myself, I live in a world of imagination and find it refreshing that my children possess this ability. But on occasion, my kids have difficulty shutting it off and returning to reality. I'll have to change my voice and sober the room by telling them Mommy and Daddy aren't playing anymore. What started as harmless is now becoming a hindrance because imagination is not something that should be without boundary.

I wonder how many of us live in the world we've created in our heads. A world of fear from things that have never happened or things people have never done. A world of "what if" and not "what is." A world of imagination going wild, robbing us of the ability to see what is real, true, and authentic. I believe imagination can be holy and helpful to break us free from the boundaries of fear—but only when tamed and filtered through self-control.

Remember Our Anchor

I, like you, can only trust myself, but that only works for a moment, not for a lifetime. My strength will eventually fade and my faith falter. But if I can remember my anchor, I can find power from a source that never runs out. You may not be a person of faith, and that's okay. But as a Christian, I believe there's only one source capable of sustaining our strength beyond our abilities, and that's hope in God the Father and his Son, Jesus Christ. In Hebrews 6:18–19, we find this written: "So God has given both his promise and his oath. These two things are unchangeable because it is impossible for God to lie. Therefore, we who have fled to him for refuge can have great confidence as we hold to the hope that lies before us. This hope is a strong and trustworthy anchor for our souls. It leads us through the curtain into God's inner sanctuary" (NLT).

I have good news for you today. Amid all the emotions life can bring, there is an anchor, a place of refuge you can run to—and that's Jesus. In him, there's hope, confidence, and an anchor for your soul. If you've felt tossed by the wind of worries of the world, can I tell you something? You're in good company. Why not join the many who searched and found something deeper than themselves to anchor to in times of emotional struggle?

There is no promise of life without pain. But there is a promise of hope within it. I hope that we all will take ownership of our emotions, consequently taking ownership of our lives. Or as I used to say to my kids, "Emotions aren't the boss of you."

Make a decision to manage your life from the inside out. Your future will thank you for it.

TWELVE

Don't Quit

"Dad, I can't do it. I just can't," were the words from my daughter when we were in line for a roller coaster at Disney World.

Our family took a surprise trip to the most magical place on earth. It was the first time for all of us, parents included. We toiled over how to tell the kids the surprise. We got custom shirts, mouse ears, and made a list of all our favorite characters. We put on Disney soundtracks and made strategic plans to hit all the right spots throughout each park.

When we arrived on our first day, we found ourselves at the first ride, a small roller coaster in Magic Kingdom. As we prepared to enter the ride, full of excitement and anticipation, my daughter panicked. She frantically began telling me and her mother that she had no desire to get on the ride.

To be honest, I was a cross between a supportive dad and skeptical investor. Disney is no cheap expense, and we didn't come to just take pictures. As we moved through the line, I went back and forth with her, coaching and calming, coaching and calming. The closer we got, the more emotional she became. Finally, I told her, "Madison, we came here to experience all the park has to offer. So today we face this fear, and if you want, you can hold on to Daddy the entire ride."

Reluctantly, she obliged. I don't think she opened her eyes once on that entire ride. Squeezing tightly, she buried her face in my chest and rode the ride reassured by my embrace. As the days went on and we went from park to park, her passion didn't grow but her participation did. What initially took tears and pep talks only took one assurance: "I'm riding with Dad."

It was almost as if she thought, "I know in his arms I won't fall out. I know in his arms I'm safe and secure." The squeezing didn't get less tight, but her eyes began to open up, tears began to dry, and even one time she lifted one hand.

Fear will do that to you in life as well. It will cause you to sit on the sideline and miss the ride. It will allow you to prepare, invest, and arrive at the cusp of all you've waited for, only to say that it's not what you thought it would be. But like Madison, we can face fears, and it doesn't have to look pretty.

Progress is not the validation of whether we did it perfectly; it's about whether we did more than before. Each day she found the courage to do a little more. And that's the call of this book—to take just one more step each day toward faith and away from fear. Your next step may require you to hold tightly to a trusted friend or to ride alone for the first time. But fear will keep you watching others when you could get on the ride.

Naturally, this is always easier said than done. We all just want to leave the pages of this book and build lives of courage and hope. And yet there are legitimate considerations we must make when preparing to do so. One of the consistent truths of history is the evolution of language. Phrases and popular clichés come and go, but now and then, something sticks. One of those phrases that has stood the test of time so far is "The struggle is real."

If you're unfamiliar, this phrase is often utilized whenever a situation, task, or season requires an extra measure of energy, patience, or strength. When asked about how they were doing after starting to work out again, I've heard someone respond with, "The struggle is real." When someone was asked what it was like having multiple children, I've heard them reply, "The struggle is real." I've heard it said as someone was recovering from a surgery or grieving the loss of a loved one. The struggle is real.

As we've walked through this book, we've witnessed that our shared experience emotionally, mentally, and physically can introduce struggle. The struggle to recover normalcy. The struggle to recover intimacy. The struggle to overcome fear, anxiety, hopelessness, and all the accompanying emotions we may find on our journey to becoming brave.

However, I believe there is a sunny side to struggle, and that is strength. At the heart of this book is a belief that bravery is not reserved for some of us, but available to all of us. But living a life beyond fear is an eternal commitment to renew, time and time again, our covenant with God and ourselves to not be overtaken by fear.

For this to be true, we must be resilient. I define *resilience* as the capacity to recover from difficulties. One definition I read said it's the ability of something to spring back into shape. In summary, resilience is about how much we can take and how quickly we can recover.

Whenever you talk about toughness and recovery, there is a temptation for misapplication. A natural urge is to imply that feelings aren't legitimate. All the more, we assume that everyone should recover from every difficulty on the same timeline and that we should project a strength that we sometimes don't possess. That is not what is intended by the paragraphs above. So, let me be clear about what resilience is not. Resilience is not the absence of emotion. It is not the avoidance of truth. It is not blind pursuits and inauthentic responses.

On the contrary, it is the capacity to process all of our realities and turn them into energy projected in the right direction as our hope. The struggle is real, and the feelings that accompany it are too.

Consequently, there is no responsible conclusion to this work that does not encourage a seasonal inspection of what I believe to be the most neglected part of our being—our soul. In a world of self-care, I dare say we're doomed without soul care.

The soul is the central part of our being that holds our exterior life (body, interactions, and experiences) and interior life (thoughts, will, and emotions) in concert together. As the ancients saw it, the soul cannot be healthy without both our exterior and interior life being fully integrated as one. In this way, integrity is the whole of life—not just individual parts—being healthy.

Soul care, then, is the continuous inspection of, investment in, and intentional commitment to a life lived in the will of God and in the ways of Jesus. Only in this can we be equipped for the life that is found beyond fear. This is why Jesus's powerful words in Mark 8:36, "What good is it for someone to gain the whole world, yet forfeit their soul?" must remain a caution for how we navigate our fears. The goal is not to find success and lose our soul. Rather, it's to let a healthy soul be the engine by which we drive our lives into the future.

The apostle Paul once again helps us with his writings to the church in Corinth. Paul understands difficulty and disappointment, change and challenges. He has experienced his fair share of struggle, and I find his voice credible in conversations about the application of resilience. Paul turns his attention on encouraging resilience in others by sharing these words:

> We are pressed on every side by troubles, but we are not crushed. We are perplexed, but not driven to despair. We are hunted down, but never abandoned by God. We get knocked down, but we are not destroyed. . . .
>
> That is why we never give up. Though our bodies are dying, our spirits are being renewed every day. For our present troubles are small and won't last very long. Yet they produce for us a glory that vastly outweighs them and will last forever! So we don't look at the troubles we can see now; rather, we fix our gaze on things that cannot be seen. For the things we see now will soon be gone, but the things we cannot see will last forever. (2 Cor. 4:8–9, 16–18 NLT)

In the Contemporary English Version, he says it like this: "We often suffer, but we are never crushed. Even when we don't know what to do, we never give up. In times of trouble, God is with us, and when we are knocked down, we get up again" (vv. 8–9).

What's interesting about Paul's approach to this particular passage is that for every reality, he offers reassurance. He beautifully captures the tension between our afflictions and our affirmations, our realities and our responses, our obstacles and our outcomes.

We suffer and feel pressure on every side, but we aren't crushed. Are we perplexed? Definitely. Confused about what to do? Surely. Are we driven to despair? Nope! Are we hunted down and experiencing troubles? Certainly. But don't we know God is with us? Yes! Have we gotten knocked down? You betcha. But we got back up again!

The lesson here is simple. The struggle is real. Nobody's refuting that, and resilience is necessary because of that truth. Resilience is about having a response to your reality.

It is not saying everything is fine, but that in everything we have a future worth fighting for.

As we face fear, a bold and brave generation stands up and decides we will not be shaken, and we will not be moved. But we should be reminded of these three simple strategies to remain resilient in what lies ahead.

Rest

I know you weren't expecting this one first. Probably because our culture has marketed resilience as what you do when you're on the battlefield, on the court, on the field, and it can certainly be expressed there as well. However, you cannot exercise resilience consistently without recovery. And you cannot experience recovery without rest.

On one particular occasion, I had the privilege of accompanying an NFL running back in a workout. If you think I was crazy to do that, you would be correct. Don't worry; there were plenty of moments where I found myself just watching, and I still feel that workout years later.

Nonetheless, I watched as he meticulously approached each segment of the workout with intentionality. First, he began by stretching. But this wasn't regular stretching; it was dynamic stretching. His version of stretching was most people's full workout. Following that, he began working through various exercises targeting specific muscle groups and professional functions. Finally, he ended with some light cardio, abs, and yet more stretching.

During the closing stretches, I began inquiring about his passion for fitness beyond the sport. It was intriguing to hear about his weekly regimen and mentality toward fitness and game preparation. He saw his body as his greatest asset. He explained how his body was like an instrument to a musician or hands to a surgeon. It functioning at its highest level week in and week out was crucial to his success. With this in mind, I asked him what part of his training regimen he deemed the most important, to which he emphatically responded, "Recovery."

Building recovery time into any training program is vital because this is when the body adapts to the stress of exercise and the actual effects of the training. Recovery also allows the body to replenish energy and repair damaged tissues. If you don't recover, you can't retain the progress made in the first place. I sat there thinking how applicable this was to any part of life—not just to the physical body but the emotional one as well. If you devalue recovery, you won't have the capacity to endure the subsequent struggle.

How well you rest will determine how hard you can run, how much you can endure, and how long you can stand in the struggle. Resilience requires recovery, and recovery requires rest. Permit yourself to recover from a season of battles and busyness. Rest is essential.

Roots

Recently, I decided to put a firepit in my backyard. As the project began, I recognized that several of the plants and trees in the area had deep roots. Once the landscaper arrived, he opened my eyes to a world beneath my feet.

Maybe you remember all of this from middle school science. However, I needed a refresher. He began sharing how the roots play an essential role for the plant because they bring water and nutrients up out of the soil and into the plant. Add to that the fact that the roots are not only suitable for the plant but good for the soil. When it rains, the roots hold the soil in place so it is not washed away. When soil does get washed away, it is called erosion.

Now, that explanation was definitely more than I asked for. Despite the beauty and wonder in all of that, I still wanted the roots gone. It did get me to think about how much erosion we might experience that would be avoided, or at least minimized, if we were adequately rooted.

Often while coaching someone through a difficult time, I'll mention this story about my backyard, and then I'll ask, "Where are your roots?" Struggle doesn't grow your roots; it reveals them. If you look hard enough and talk long enough, they always show up. Your response reveals your roots.

What's feeding your heart? What is your mind living off of? What's holding everything together? Good, bad, or neutral, we all have roots. And they usually show up in three ways: principles, people, and places.

Paul speaks to this in Colossians 2:6–7: "So then, just as you received Christ Jesus as Lord, continue to live your lives in him, rooted and built up in him, strengthened in the faith as you were taught, and overflowing with thankfulness."

The New Living Translation says, "Let your roots grow down into him, and let your lives be built on him. Then your faith will grow strong in the truth you were taught, and you will overflow with thankfulness" (v. 7).

This passage in Jeremiah 17 paints a powerful picture as well:

> But blessed is the man who trusts me, GOD,
> the woman who sticks with GOD.

> They're like trees replanted in Eden,
>   putting down roots near the rivers—
> Never a worry through the hottest of summers,
>   never dropping a leaf,
> Serene and calm through droughts,
>   bearing fresh fruit every season. (vv. 7–8 MSG)

What an image, what an aspiration. Being serene and calm through droughts can be paralleled to all these moments we've referenced throughout this book. A drought could mean a season of disappointment, loss, unmet expectations, or financial difficulty.

As a person of faith, I believe that being rooted in Christ and his promises is a firm foundation, and it gives me hope in hard times and strength in weak moments. In addition to our faith, vital friendships serve to reinforce our endurance and support. We need people we can rely on to handle our truth, hold our hand, and help us move forward. And we have environments that we need to manage in difficult moments, simply because they don't deposit but deplete. Knowing how these show up in our life is essential to our success in the struggle.

Before we can develop resilience, we first have to ensure our resilience is properly rooted. Here are four questions you may consider when thinking of this.

1. How does my faith inform my response to struggle? (Principles)
2. Who are the three people I trust the most in times of crisis or seasons of struggle? (People)
3. What environments or places make me feel most refilled and recovered? (Places)
4. Of the answers above, where might I need to consider revision or replacement to have healthier roots?

Reminders

This may seem like a stretch, but walk with me here. Do you know what gives me confidence when I get nervous when I'm about to speak in front of a group of people? I tell myself, "Vernon, you've done this before."

Do you know what I rely on when I'm overwhelmed before making a big decision? "Vernon, you've done this before."

Do you know how I pull myself together when I have to get another surgery on my leg? "Vernon, you've done this before."

Do you know what I think when our toilet breaks, and I'm not a plumber at all, but it's got to get done? "Vernon, you've done this before."

Okay, I got a little help on that last one, and my wife would probably prefer from here on out I call an actual plumber. But the point is, when I remind myself of what I have done, overcome, and conquered, it retrains my brain to see not only the struggle but the history that preceded it. It is in history that I find hope to endure the present.

Now, I don't know if fixing toilets is a struggle for you, and you may not have an illness, but wherever you see a challenge before you, remind yourself of all the times you've done this before. Remind yourself of all the times your resilience showed up to see you through another trying season. I'd bet you have some strength in your story that, when summoned to the forefront, will become a faith filler for your future. If you want to go a step further, make these reminders visible—post them on the refrigerator. Place a picture on the nightstand. Put something on the dashboard of your car. Remind yourself, "I've done this before!" The reminders of resilience can become a catalyst to hope and endurance for your future.

The struggle may be real. But there is a response to your reality; we find endurance to win again with the right principles, people, and places.

I can't promise perfection. But I can promise purpose always emerges in progress. Wherever you're headed on the other side of this book, do me a favor and fail for it, stretch for it, believe for it, fight for it. It doesn't matter how long it takes or where it leads. A life of hope is so much better than a life of fear.

In college, I learned this poem by Edgar Albert Guest, and it has been a staple when fear is getting the best of me. I hope it encourages you.

Don't Quit

When things go wrong, as they sometimes will,
When the road you're trudging seems all uphill,
When the funds are low and the debts are high,
And you want to smile, but you have to sigh,
When care is pressing you down a bit—
Rest, if you must, but don't you quit.

Life is strange with its twists and turns,
As every one of us sometimes learns,
And many a fellow turns about,
When he might have won had he stuck it out;
Don't give up though the pace seems slow—
You may succeed with another blow.

Often the goal is nearer than
It seems to a faint and faltering man,
Often the struggler has given up
When he might have captured the victor's cup,
And he learned too late when the night came down,
How close he was to the golden crown.

> Success is failure turned inside out—
> The silver tint of the clouds of doubt,
> And you never can tell how close you are,
> It may be near when it seems so far;
> So stick to the fight when you're hardest hit—
> It's when things seem worst that you must not quit.[1]

That's what I'd love to leave you with. Don't quit. Our world needs more brave and more bold people who are willing to pursue a future beyond their fears. I believe you are one of those people.

And every day won't feel the same. But don't quit! Be brave. Be bold. We need what you bring to the world. Welcome to a life beyond your fears.

Acknowledgments

To my wife, Ashley. Since we were sixteen years old, your love, wisdom, and honesty have helped me become who I am today. Your fingerprints are on these pages as well, as we've faced many of our fears together.

To my miracles, Madison and Jackson. Being your dad is one of my greatest honors. I hope this book is a North Star for you one day as you face your own fears and unlock your personal courage. Thank you for sharing your dad with the world by giving me both time and inspiration to write.

To my parents, who first unlocked the wonder of words for me. I appreciate you shaping me into the man I am today. And thank you for always encouraging me to communicate my thoughts, ideas, and lessons out loud. I am because you are.

To my agent, Don Gates. Thank you for taking a call with a guy you'd never met. For giving me hard questions and hard truths. But, most importantly, for believing in me, this message, and this moment. You have been a valuable guide in climbing this new mountain, and I am eternally grateful.

To the team at Baker Publishing. I can't say thank you enough. Your belief in me as a writer, your support at every stage, and your passion behind this project have opened a world of possibility to me. Being part of the team is an honor, and I'm so excited for this moment. A special thank you to Rachel McRae. You were more than an editor—you were a bridge from the unknown into a new world. From the first conversation, you made me believe this book mattered and that I didn't have to discover this new world alone. You'll never know how much your guiding presence meant to me.

To Tony Dungy. Thank you for always making time to invite my family into your family. Your example above all else has marked my life in ways I could never fully articulate. Thank you for lending your words to this moment in my life.

To the greatest church in the world, The Life Church. Thank you for taking countless journeys with me over the years. I hope you know that the journey to bring the message of *life* to the world is one we do together. I pray you see this book as another step for *us* bringing that mission to life.

Lastly, to the kid who has cancer or is going through some other challenging moment right now, wondering what life looks like on the other side. Keep living, keep dreaming, keep fighting. Your story is still being written, and we need the chapters that are yet to unfold. Thank you in advance for not giving up, because your story will change the world one day.

Notes

Chapter 1 The Bigger They Are, the Quieter They Fall

1. J. K. Rowling, "Text of J.K. Rowling's Speech," *Harvard Gazette*, June 5, 2008, https://news.harvard.edu/gazette/story/2008/06/text-of-j-k-rowling-speech/.

Chapter 2 The Faces of Fear

1. "Love Yourz," track 12 on J. Cole, *2014 Forest Hills Drive*, Columbia Records, 2014.

Chapter 4 Fear Is Not Hard to Find

1. Chapman University, "The Chapman Survey of American Fears, Wave 9: The Complete List of Fears, 2023," 2023, https://www.chapman.edu/wilkinson/research-centers/babbie-center/_files/2023%20Fear/23csaf-9_high-to-low.pdf.
2. Christopher D. Bader et al., *Fear Itself: The Causes and Consequences of Fear in America* (NYU Press, 2020).
3. American Psychiatric Association, *Diagnostic and Statistical Manual of Mental Disorders 5-TR* (APA, 2022), 215.
4. Jonathan Haidt, *The Anxious Generation: How the Great Rewiring of Childhood Is Causing an Epidemic of Mental Illness* (Penguin Press, 2024), 27.
5. Haidt, *Anxious Generation*, 27.

Chapter 5 Winning the War Against Worry

1. Paul Baines et al., *Sage Handbook of Propaganda* (Sage Publications, 2019), 79.

Notes

Chapter 7 Somewhere Over the Rainbow

1. Theodore Roosevelt, "The Man in the Arena," Theodore Roosevelt Center at Dickson State University, April 23, 1910, https://www.theo dorerooseveltcenter.org/Learn-About-TR/TR-Encyclopedia/Culture-and -Society/Man-in-the-Arena.aspx.

2. "Over the Rainbow," by Yip Harburg and Harold Arlen, Leo Feist, Inc., 1939.

Chapter 8 Power to the People

1. Brené Brown, "The Power of Vulnerability," posted January 3, 2011, by TED, YouTube, https://www.youtube.com/watch?v=iCvmsMzlF7o.

Chapter 9 No Guts, No Glory

1. Frederick Blesse, *No Guts, No Glory,* April 1, 1975, https://simhq .net/_air/PDF/NGNG.pdf.

Chapter 10 Higher Ground

1. Elisa Shearer, "More Than Eight in Ten Americans Get News from Digital Devices," Pew Research Center, January 12, 2021, https://www .pewresearch.org/short-reads/2021/01/12/more-than-eight-in-ten-ameri cans-get-news-from-digital-devices/.

2. F. P. Putri and N. Dewi, "Growth Monitoring of Koi Fish (*Cyprinus caprio*) in Natural Hatchery Techniques, in Umbulan, Pasauruan, East Java," *IOP Conference Series: Earth and Environmental Science* 236 (October 2018), https://iopscience.iop.org/article/10.1088/1755-1315 /236/1/012016.

Chapter 11 Inside Out

1. T. K. Coleman et al., *Freedom Without Permission: How to Live Free in a World That Isn't* (CreateSpace Independent Publishing, 2015), 19.

2. Brené Brown, *Daring Greatly: How the Courage to Be Vulnerable Transforms the Way We Live, Love, Parent, and Lead* (Avery, 2015), 2.

Chapter 12 Don't Quit

1. Edgar Albert Guest, "Don't Quit," *Detroit Free Press*, 1921.

VERNON GORDON is a leadership consultant and a sought-after speaker who serves as the lead/founding pastor of The Life Church in Virginia, one of the fastest growing churches in America. He is the founder of The Mosaic Project, a nonprofit created to inspire social change and cultural unity for the greater good through content and coaching. Cofounder with his wife of Gordon Solutions, a leadership consulting firm, Gordon earned his MDiv from the Samuel DeWitt Proctor School of Theology of Virginia Union University. Vernon is married to his high school sweetheart, Ashley, and they have two children, Madison and Jackson.

CONNECT WITH VERNON

VernonGordon.com

Vernon Gordon   vernongordon

A Note from the Publisher

Dear Reader,

Thank you for selecting a Revell book! We're so happy to be part of your life through this work.

Revell's mission is to publish books that offer hope and help for meeting life's challenges, and that bring comfort and inspiration. We know that the right words at the right time can make all the difference; it is our goal with every title to provide just the words you need.

We believe in building lasting relationships with readers, and we'd love to get to know you better. If you have any feedback, questions, or just want to chat about your experience reading this book, please email us directly at publisher@revellbooks.com. Your insights are incredibly important to us, and it would be our pleasure to hear how we can better serve you.

We look forward to hearing from you and having the chance to enhance your experience with Revell Books.

The Publishing Team at Revell Books
A Division of Baker Publishing Group
publisher@revellbooks.com

Revell